The SECURE SOUL

Companion Guide

DR. ALISON COOK

W Publishing Group
An Imprint of Thomas Nelson

The Secure Soul Companion Guide

Published in Nashville, Tennessee, by W Publishing, an imprint of Thomas Nelson.

The author is represented by Alive Literary Agency, www.aliveliterary.com.

ISBN 978-1-4003-5262-3 (audiobook)
ISBN 978-1-4003-5261-6 (eBook)
ISBN 978-1-4003-5260-9 (TP)

Library of Congress Control Number:

Printed in the United States of America

26 27 28 29 30 LBC 5 4 3 2 1

A NOTE FROM DR. ALISON

Dear Soul Mender,

I'm so glad you're here. Truly. As you open these pages, I want you to know this: Every reflection you'll find here has been crafted with you in mind. I pictured you as I wrote each one. I thought about your desire for inner security, your ache to feel whole, your longing to know God's loving presence more intimately.

For years I struggled with deep insecurity and even self-contempt. The practices you'll find in these pages—reconnecting with every part of your soul and welcoming each one into God's loving presence—have slowly changed me. Over time, I've discovered a grounded, steady strength within, a kindness toward myself I once thought impossible, and a genuine affection for the unique person God has shaped me to be. And I've learned something beautiful along the way: The more secure my inner world becomes, the more freely I can build relationships marked by trust, joy, and authentic connection.

This is the slow, steady work of becoming a secure soul. And it's never something we do alone. It's part you—bringing awareness, honesty, and your story. And it's part God—bringing presence, healing, and love into the very places that long for wholeness.

And this workbook, a companion guide to *The Secure Soul*, is meant to help you practice exactly that.

The pages that follow are designed as a series of short, guided reflections you can enter into whenever you need to steady yourself. You can think of these reflections as steps on a journey toward a more secure soul. They are meant to help you bring what you're learning about your own story into your spiritual practices, cultivating growth and healing that deepens and takes root. Each one is short, just ten to fifteen minutes. You can work through them on your own, each day in the quiet of your own soul with God; or you can work through them with a trusted friend, small group, mentor, or therapist.

This companion guide is divided into two parts.

Part One: Finding Inner Strength and Connection is designed to be read in sequence. Each reflection builds on the one before, leading you step-by-step into deeper awareness of your inner world and into the steadying presence of God. Think of this first section as the root system, the essential grounding every soul needs.

Part Two: Love Notes to Secure Your Soul is different. You don't need to move through it in order. Instead, think of it as a collection of love notes to your soul—words you can return to whenever trust feels hard—when conflict flares, when loneliness stings, when criticism lands deep, or when you simply feel far from God. You can read these notes as if they're from the wisest part of yourself, or you might imagine them coming from the parent you wish you'd had, from me, or even from God. In addition to each love note, you'll find two sections to help you engage more personally: A Pause for the Soul, with space to reflect; and Going Deeper exercises. These sections are here for you, offering a way back to safety, presence, and love in the moments when fear rises up.

This work isn't about fixing yourself. It's about slowing down long enough to listen to the cries of your soul, to notice where old stories still live, and to discover the God who has always been right there with you, even when you have felt most alone.

As you engage these pages—looking back at your past, noticing what's happening today, and imagining a future rooted in secure love—your soul will slowly become like a tree planted by streams of water, anchored in Love, resilient in hardship, and fruitful in its season (Ps. 1:3).

This is my prayer for you: that every page becomes another root stretching deep into the soil of God's unshakable love.

With you on the journey,
Alison

PART ONE, SECTION 1

FINDING INNER STRENGTH AND CONNECTION

The Roots of Disconnection

STEP 1

ARRIVE WHERE YOU ARE

We all know the ache of disconnection, of feeling alone even in a room full of people, far from belonging, far from love itself. Maybe you feel it at work where no one really sees you. Or in a community where you've shown up faithfully and yet still can't quite find your people. Maybe you feel it in your family, in your friendships, or even in your marriage.

Every soul carries stories—stories of connection and safety, and also stories of loss, longing, and disconnection. These stories live in your body, your longings, your fears, and the patterns you return to without even realizing it. And the work of becoming a secure soul begins right here, not by revisiting the past but by learning to arrive where you are.

Arriving where you are means bringing your real self into the present moment—your honest thoughts, emotions, longings, and needs—and letting God meet you there. This can feel uncomfortable at first, because the moment we stop and get honest, we often notice what we'd rather avoid: fear, shame, sorrow, or the pull to distract ourselves.

But this discomfort isn't proof of your failure. *It's proof of your humanity.* And meeting yourself right here with compassion, paradoxically, is the path back toward connection and belonging.

Psychologists often describe the pain of disconnection as an attachment wound. It's like an alarm in the soul that flares when we don't feel safe, seen, or held. Theologians call it the wound of the fall, echoing the ancient ache that began when we first experienced rupture with the Source of Love itself.

The creation story tells us that, in the beginning, the garden pulsed with life. Adam and Eve walked in harmony, fully at home with God, with themselves, and with one another. There was no fear, no hiding, no shame. This is the ultimate picture of security, safety, and loving connectedness.

But when they reached for the fruit, something broke. Not only trust with God, but trust with each other and trust *within* themselves. Suddenly, their bodies felt exposed. Their eyes darted away from each other. What once felt safe now felt threatening.

When they heard God's footsteps, they hid. The One who had always been a source of companionship now felt like a source of danger. "I was afraid," Adam admitted, "so I hid" (Gen. 3:10).

This ancient story reveals the essence of disconnection.

- Disconnection from God: *Shame replaces intimacy.*
- Disconnection from self: *Fear replaces confidence.*
- Disconnection from others: *Blame replaces trust.*

The ache of Genesis 3 isn't about breaking a rule. It's about breaking *connection.* A world once alive with love and belonging fractured into hiding, fear, and isolation. And we've all inherited that ache, that sense of disconnection.

And yet, even here, God finds us. "Where are you?" God asks gently. In his beautiful book *Healing What's Within*, therapist and spiritual director Chuck DeGroat helps us see that God asks this question not to shame us but because *he longs to reconnect with us.*[1] It's a question rooted in love.

Where are you, my beloved?

No matter where you are, I am here with you.

You can always return to Love.

RECOGNIZE DISCONNECTION

1. Recall a time recently when you felt disconnected from yourself, from another person, or from God. Note briefly what happened.

2. What did you feel in that moment?

3. What messages did you tell yourself?

RETURN TO LOVE

Imagine God speaking your name with tenderness: (insert your name), *where are you?*

Simply notice what surfaces without judgment. Then, write a few sentences in response to God's question.

1. What fears or longings surface as you sit with that question?

STEP 2

NAME THE PAIN OF NOT BEING CHOSEN

Just the other day, a friend reached out to me. She was in tears, grieving the emotional distance she felt from her husband.

"He's a good man," she said. "Loyal. Faithful. But he won't let me in, nor does he seem to want to know more about me. I've grown so much in understanding myself. And all that growth is leading to a feeling of *more* distance with him."

Her words were honest. Brave. And achingly familiar.

The pain of not being chosen shows up in countless ways. Sometimes it's outright rejection. Other times, it's more subtle. It might show up as the feeling of being unseen, overlooked, or not fully let in. Reflections on this kind of ache are among the most common I hear from clients, friends, even strangers. And I've felt this ache deeply within myself.

Do any of these resonate with you?

- *I reach for my spouse, but he shuts down or changes the subject.*
- *I try to tell my mom what I'm going through, but she redirects to her own story.*
- *I ask my child how she's doing, and she shrugs me off without even looking up.*
- *I try to connect with a friend group, only to feel like they don't really care if I'm around.*

These moments are so painful.

And yet—they're also sacred.

Why? Because they reveal that your soul is *intact.* Your soul was designed for connection. When you notice that pang of rejection, of being unseen or not chosen, it's a signal that something inside you is *alive.* It's your soul reaching, longing for what God always intended for you—the warmth and safety of love that holds steady, a love that *always* invites you in.

Not feeling chosen hurts because you were made for belonging. That ache that you feel is a sign that your soul has not given up!

And here's the good news: Healing that ache for connection doesn't mean minimizing what happened, and it doesn't require fixing the other person. It begins by recognizing the part of *you* that is longing, offering yourself kindness, and then opening that tender place within to God's loving presence.

RECOGNIZE THE PAIN OF NOT BEING CHOSEN

Think of a recent moment when you felt the sting of rejection—when you felt unseen, overlooked, or not fully embraced.

1. What emotions rise up as you revisit this moment?

2. What do you notice in your body?

Stay here for a moment. Let yourself witness the ache of your soul—not as failure, but as evidence of life inside you.

RETURN TO LOVE

In Psalm 42:5, the psalmist speaks directly to his own soul: “Why, my soul, are you downcast? Why so disturbed within me? Put your hope in God, for I will yet praise him, my Savior and my God.”

Imagine this not as a scolding but as a tender dialogue.

1. What word best captures “downcast” for you right now (heavy, lonely, restless, empty)?

2. Now rewrite Psalm 42:5 in your own words—with honesty and with hope. Speak to your soul the way you would speak to someone you love.

STEP 3

RECOGNIZE SOUL RUPTURES

There's a particular ache that comes with disconnection—the sting of not being chosen and the deeper longing that reveals your soul was made for love.

Those moments of disconnection are rarely just about what's happening right now. More often, they reverberate through your inner world, echoing with memories of other times you've felt left out, misunderstood, or unseen. What seems small in the present can awaken a much older ache. Suddenly, you're flooded with emotions that feel far bigger than the moment at hand.

I call this a *soul rupture*: the inner experience of your heart sinking or splitting open. It's that moment when something in you breaks loose, leaving you aching not only for connection with others but also for a sense of safety within yourself. It's a rupture that doesn't just speak of today's hurt but taps on wounds that came before, leaving you caught in pain that is both present and past.

In moments like these, you might notice old messages echoing through your soul:

- *No one really gets me.*
- *People always leave me.*
- *I'm too much.*
- *No matter what I do, it will never be good enough.*
- *I'll always be on my own.*

Here's the paradox: These very messages that are so painful also carry the doorway to healing. Each time you become aware of one of these messages—each time you notice the old refrain rising up—you are also given the chance to respond differently. Awareness itself becomes an invitation to tend to the tear inside your own soul, to reanchor in Love, and to slowly create a more secure base within.

Each time you pause to recognize a soul rupture and return to Love in that moment, you're engaging in real soul mending. Both Scripture and science point us here:

- Science calls it *neuroplasticity*: your brain's ability to change and rewire old messages over time.
- Scripture calls it *being renewed in your inner person* (2 Cor. 4:16): the slow, steady transformation that happens as you open your whole self to God.

Together, they invite us into a sacred rhythm: recognizing disconnection and returning to God's loving presence—a rhythm that, when practiced over time, begins to mend the tears within.

RECOGNIZE A SOUL RUPTURE

Consider a recent moment when an ache rose up inside you. Maybe a silence that stung, a comment that cut deeper than expected, or a moment of feeling invisible or unseen.

1. What thoughts or feelings do you notice?

2. What are you longing for?

3. How are you tempted to protect yourself (shut down, avoid, defend)?

Linger here for a moment. Let yourself witness the stirring in your soul, not as a problem to fix but as evidence of a place within your soul that needs tending.

RETURN TO LOVE

Imagine the wisest version of yourself sitting with this hurting part of you. Or, if it's helpful, you might picture God, or someone who embodies care—someone who has shown you what it feels like to be truly seen.

1. What do you sense your soul needs to hear in this moment? Write a phrase or draw an image that comes to mind:

Take a moment to linger here. Simply notice what it's like to stay with your soul. As you stay with yourself, you're forming new attachment tethers *within*—threads of love linking you to the hurting places inside and to the One who never leaves, no matter what you're going through.

Finally, end with gratitude. Write your own prayer of thanks, or let these words guide you:

God, thank you that I don't have to carry this alone. You see me, even in the torn places. You are with me here. You are renewing me in ways I cannot always see.

STEP 4

MAP YOUR ATTACHMENT STYLE

Over the past few days, you've begun to notice the ache of disconnection and the inner rupture it creates within your soul. You've recognized what disconnection feels like and practiced turning toward that ache with compassion. But the truth is, that ache doesn't stay contained inside us. It spills over into how we reach for others.

For some of us, disconnection stirs up a whirlwind. We feel panicky or restless inside, wondering what we did wrong. We may try harder to bridge the distance: sending another text, explaining ourselves, raising our voices, or reaching out for reassurances.

For others, disconnection brings a wall. We shut down. We retreat into silence, or distract ourselves with work, scrolling, or busyness. We tell ourselves: *I don't care. It doesn't matter.*

For most of us, it's a combination of both. These responses aren't who you are. They're how your nervous system learned to respond when connection felt threatened.

Psychologists often describe these tendencies as *anxious* and *avoidant* patterns of attachment.

Anxious responses look like:

- Pursuing closeness when the other pulls away
- Overexplaining or defending yourself
- People-pleasing to keep the peace
- Worrying constantly about what others think
- Feeling panicked at the thought of disconnection

Avoidant responses look like:

- Withdrawing when emotions rise
- Downplaying or minimizing your needs
- Shutting down feelings to stay in control
- Distracting yourself or staying busy to avoid vulnerability
- Trying to appear "fine" on the outside while feeling anything but fine on the inside

None of these responses is wrong. They're cues that your soul is in distress—bids for connection from deep within.

For many of us, these patterns begin early in life. When connection felt uncertain, your nervous system learned ways to reach for closeness or protect you from hurt. Each response is rooted in a deep longing to feel safe, seen, and loved.

Recognizing your own pattern isn't about blaming yourself. It's about becoming *more compassionate toward yourself.* When you notice your go-to response, you can gently remind yourself: *This makes sense. I learned this once to stay safe. And now I can learn a new way.*

RECOGNIZE YOUR ATTACHMENT STYLE

Think back to a recent moment when you felt disconnected from, hurt by, or in conflict with a friend, loved one, or colleague. See if you can tap in to what that moment stirred up within your soul.

1. What feelings rose up inside you (anxiety, fear, shame, frustration, etc.)?

2. How did you try to create safety for yourself in that moment, whether through reaching out or pulling back (pleasing, pursuing, overexplaining, withdrawing, shutting down, etc.)?

3. What messages did you tell yourself to make sense of what was happening? (Anxious: *I have to fix this.* Avoidant: *It doesn't matter. I'm fine.*)

4. What fears surface if you imagine *not* responding in this way?

5. Notice what this reveals about how your soul responds in moments of disconnection.

When I feel disconnected, I tend to:

This usually sounds like me saying or doing:

RETURN TO LOVE

Close your eyes and picture a safe place, a place where you feel clearheaded, light, secure, held in Love.

1. Take a moment to jot down what you pictured. Where are you? What are you doing?

2. What do you notice in your body as you connect with this sense of safety?

3. If it's helpful, pause and consider what it's like to connect with God's presence here. What do you notice?

4. Write one grounding truth you want to carry with you.

Each time you pause with gentleness instead of reacting, you begin carving a new pathway back to connection—with yourself, with God, and with other people.

STEP 5

TRACE YOUR FIRST PATTERNS OF LOVE

You've started to notice how you tend to respond in moments of disconnection, either by leaning in anxiously or pulling away to protect yourself. Those responses don't come out of nowhere. Every pattern has a story. The question is: *Where did yours begin?*

None of us wakes up one day and decides, "I'll be the one who chases," or "I'll be the one who hides." These responses were formed long ago, usually in the relationships that first taught us what love felt like.

Before you had words, before you could even remember, you were already learning:

- Is love reliable?
- When I reach out, will someone come close?
- When I cry, will someone comfort me—or turn away?

Those early experiences became the blueprint for how you respond to disconnection or discomfort today. Your current attachment patterns are formed in your earliest relationships, the places where the tapestry of love and connectedness first began to shape your soul.

You may have had your physical needs for food, clothing, and shelter met. But those things alone don't create secure attachment. What fosters true inner security is *presence*—someone who noticed your spoken and unspoken cues, delighted in you, held you when you were hurting, and came back to repair when something went wrong.

When those moments of disconnection weren't noticed or repaired, something inside you learned to guard against disappointment. You may have learned to read the room, to anticipate others' moods, to hold back your true feelings, or to work harder for love that felt just out of reach. Or you learned to stay busy, stay independent, or stay numb.

But here's the good news: Attachment patterns are not set in concrete. Even if you didn't experience consistent support or loving presence as a child, your soul can still learn what safety feels like. Psychologists calls this "earned security": the ability to grow in secure attachment later in life through trustworthy relationships. And at the very center of this healing is your relationship with God, the ultimate source of steady, unwavering, loving attachment.

RECOGNIZE EARLY PATTERNS

Create a simple map of your first attachment figures. You might include parents, step-parents, siblings, grandparents, teachers, coaches, family friends, or other caregivers who helped shape what love felt like. Place each person on the page however it feels natural. For example, you might place each person closer or farther from you, group people by season of life, or simply list them.

Under each person's name, write a word or short phrase that captures what it felt like to be with them back then—whether it was mostly safe, mixed, or mostly unsafe. This exercise isn't about laying blame. It's about noticing what love felt like to you early on, and how your soul learned to adapt. For example:

- *Present in practical ways . . . less available emotionally.*
- *Safe much of the time . . . unpredictable when stressed.*
- *Absent or neglectful . . . I felt alone with my feelings.*
- *Caring and loving . . . and had limits they couldn't get past.*
- *Critical or controlling . . . my needs weren't welcome.*
- *Comforting in crisis . . . distant in everyday moments.*

My Attachment Map

This map reveals your first attachment tethers: the threads that shaped your early sense of security and belonging. It helps you see how your experience of connectedness was woven in the beginning.

1. When did you feel most safe as a child? When did you feel least safe?

2. How did your caregivers respond when you were sad, scared, or in need of comfort?

3. How was conflict handled in your family (apologies, forgiveness, minimization, explosions, etc.)?

4. What did you learn to do when you had a need (ask for help, hide, get angry, stay quiet, etc.)?

5. Who was the first person who made you feel truly safe?

RETURN TO LOVE

Now look at your map and what you've written. Notice the strong threads, as well as the ones that are torn. Place your hand over the part of the map that feels the most tender or frayed.

1. What do you notice in your own soul as you look at that name or memory?

Imagine sitting beside your younger self in that moment, or picture God there with you, if it's helpful. Psalm 147:3 says, "He heals the brokenhearted and binds up their wounds."

2. The words my younger self needs to hear are:

Let this blessing settle over you:
I am here.
God is here.
I am not alone.
Even the torn places can be rewoven in love.

This is how healing begins—by letting Love return to the places that first learned to fear, to hide, or to work overtime to hold everything together.

STEP 6

IDENTIFY THE ROLES YOU LEARNED

Every family is its own ecosystem—a living network of interconnected parts. Think of an orchestra or choir and how each member plays a vital role. When everyone stays grounded in their own strengths *and* attuned to the conductor, something beautiful emerges. The music isn't perfect. There are missed notes and moments of tension. But overall there is harmony. Each person belongs, and everyone understands their place in the larger whole.

Likewise, in healthy families, everyone has a voice, and everyone can also step back to let others be heard. Differences are respected, and one person's needs or preferences don't dominate all the others. At the same time, compromise is essential. Each person recognizes that from time to time, they'll need to bend so that the whole can remain strong. When conflict arises—as it will—wise parents guide the family back toward connection through honesty, accountability, and repair.

In less healthy families, however, the music falters. The rhythm breaks down. In some homes, there is no music at all, just a cacophony of noise or a deafening silence. Every family has its challenges, but when a home loses its rhythm—whether through small moments of disconnection or through deep instability—*children instinctively adapt.* They take on roles, big or small, to hold the fragments together as best they can.

One child might work overtime to hold everything together, while another fades into the background unheard. These roles aren't signs of weakness. They are the soul's way of seeking safety when love feels unpredictable. But over time they leave lasting marks on your identity and ongoing patterns of connectedness.

Six common roles children can fall into are:[1]

- **The Golden Child**—the one who can do no wrong. You learned to do whatever it took to earn praise and admiration, without recognizing the cost—a crushing pressure to succeed and difficulty tolerating failure or disappointment.
- **The Comedian**—the one who lightens the room with a joke. You learned to make laughter your shield against conflict. But behind the smile, you often hid the pain you didn't feel safe enough to share.
- **The Scapegoat**—the one who carries the family's problems. You were branded as the problem, or the difficult one, even though you were simply telling the truth or refusing to play along. Your creativity and honesty got buried under blame.
- **The Invisible One**—the quiet child who stays out of the way. You learned to avoid trouble, but you also missed out on being known. Growing up unseen, you often internalized the message *I don't matter.*
- **The Caretaker**—the one who steps into adult shoes too soon. You learned to become the peacemaker, the helper, the responsible one. But the weight of carrying others left you vulnerable to exhaustion, codependency, and neglecting your own needs.
- **The Rebel**—the one who pushes back against family rules. Often misunderstood, you resisted as your way of signaling unmet needs. Beneath the defiance, there was usually a longing to be recognized and understood.

Most of us will recognize ourselves in at least one of these roles, sometimes more. The key is not to criticize or blame but to get curious:

What role did I play?

What did it cost me?

What did it teach me about how I show up in my adult relationships?

RECOGNIZE THE ROLES YOU PLAYED

1. Review the list of six common family roles above. Which role or roles do you most identify with in your family of origin?

2. When you think back to your role in the family, how did your role lead to a feeling of love or safety?

3. In what ways did this role get rewarded, and what was the cost to you?

4. How does this role—both its benefits and its costs—still show up in your adult relationships?

RETURN TO LOVE

Now gently return to the awareness that God is already with you in the places where old patterns still touch your present life. Write out your own prayer, or lean on the words in this one:

God, thank you for how this role helped me survive.
But I am more than this role.
Show me how to step into the fullness of who you made me to be.
Teach me what it means that all of me can show up in the safety of your love.

1. What aspect of this role do you sense a nudge to release?

2. What aspect of this role would you like to keep—but not at the expense of your own needs, rest, or wholeness?

3. Reflect on the following verse: "The LORD is my shepherd, I lack nothing. . . . He refreshes my soul" (Ps. 23:1, 3). If God were restoring your soul in this place, what might that look like today?

Awareness opens the door to love. Love is what transforms us.

STEP 7

ANCHOR IN GOD AS YOUR SECURE BASE

The roles you carried when you were young didn't just shape how you related to parents or siblings, or even how you relate to others today. They also shape how you relate to God. For example:

- If you were the Golden Child, you may hustle to prove yourself worthy of God's delight, fearing his love could slip away if you don't measure up.
- If you were the Invisible One, you may assume God overlooks you, believing he's more concerned with others than with you.
- If you were the Scapegoat, you may brace for God's displeasure, expecting blame—or pushing that blame back onto him.
- If you were the Caretaker, you may feel close to God when you're caring for others while losing touch with your own needs.
- If you were the Rebel, you may keep God at a distance, expecting criticism, rejection, shame, or abandonment.
- If you were the Comedian, you may use humor or distraction to keep God from seeing the depth of your pain.

And yet, the good news is this: God is big enough to meet you in the very contours of these wounds. God's love is not one-size-fits-all. It is personal, intimate, and tenderly attuned to your unique story.

This is why healing can't stop with identifying your roles, or even with building healthier patterns in your present life. Those things matter. But we also need a deeper kind of attachment—one that reaches beyond what even the best human relationships can hold. We need to encounter a God who doesn't ask us to play a role at all.

God is not your parents, your teachers, or your past relationships. Most of us understand this cognitively. But to experience God as God really is, we often need to notice where those old wounds still cloud the picture of what God's love is really like.

Healing begins as you let God meet you inside those younger places in your soul where you learned to perform, disappear, stay guarded, or carry blame. Little by little, you discover a different kind of attachment: steady, personal, and safe. A secure base.

This is where the real God meets you—not as a projection of old wounds or unmet needs but as the steady, healing Presence who moves toward you in them.

The One who sees you.

The One who holds you.

The One who stays.

The ultimate source of Love.

RECOGNIZE WOUNDED IMAGES OF GOD

1. Take a few minutes to journal about the earliest sense of God you remember. Did you experience God as near or distant? Gentle or stern? Demanding or kind?

2. Now write about how you experience God today. Is the picture the same, or has it shifted? Where do you notice growth, and where do old feelings still linger?

3. Looking back at your family of origin, do you notice any parallels? Does your current image of God resemble the way a parent, caregiver, or family role once made you feel—overlooked, unprotected, pressured, blamed, or delighted in?

Imagine your soul as a house with two rooms.

Room One:
This is where your earliest images of love and safety—or the lack of love and safety—live. Picture it. Maybe the air feels tense, or the light is dim. Maybe love felt conditional: safe one moment, distant the next. Maybe you're safe but alone in a room that feels sparsely furnished. Take a moment to jot down a few words or images that describe this room, or sketch a simple picture of it if you'd like.

Room Two:
Now imagine God gently opening the door to another room. This space feels different. It's spacious, steady, warm. Here, you don't have to perform. You don't have to disappear. You are seen and loved just as you are. What does the light look like in this room? What colors or furnishings are here? Let Jesus' words guide you: "My Father will love them, and we will come to them and make our home with them" (John 14:23). Write down a few words or images that describe this second room, or draw it if you'd like.

1. How often do you still find yourself in Room One?

2. What does it feel like when you allow yourself to settle into Room Two—into the home God is making in your soul?

RETURN TO LOVE

Choose one scripture about God's nearness, goodness, gentleness, or kindness (like Ps. 34:18; Isa. 41:10; 1 John 4:7). Rewrite it as if God were speaking directly to you.

For example:

Psalm 34:18: *(Insert your name), I am close to you in your heartbreak. I see your crushed spirit, and I will hold you.*

Slowly read your version aloud as if you are speaking directly to your own soul. What shifts within you?

This week, pay attention to small moments of safety. It might be as simple as a friend's kindness, a quiet walk, or a warm cup of tea. When they come, pause and remind your soul: *This is what God's love feels like. Steady. Gentle. Present.*

Slowly, moment by moment, you are teaching your soul the truth: You are *already held* by the steady, anchoring presence of a God who is *for* you.

PART ONE, SECTION 2

FINDING INNER STRENGTH AND CONNECTION

Strengthening Your Inner Soul

STEP 8

SHIFT FROM OUTER ROLES TO INNER PATTERNS

In your family, you learned certain roles to stay connected, certain ways of earning love, avoiding conflict, or protecting yourself from hurt. Those roles didn't vanish with adulthood. Over time, they settled into your inner world as familiar patterns. These patterns shape tender, young places within you that still rise up when something feels uncertain.

That's why you may sometimes feel confused by your own reactions—responses that seem far bigger than the situation at hand:

- A small critique from a colleague leaves you panicked.
- A spouse walks away in conflict and suddenly you feel abandoned.
- You scroll or snack late at night, then wake up wondering why you sabotaged yourself.

These are inner bids for connection. They're signals from within that something in you is looking for safety, reassurance, comfort, or care.

In *The Secure Soul*, we explored three recurring patterns that often show up as distinct (but interconnected) voices—or parts—within us:

- The Controller: the part of your soul who learned that safety meant staying self-sufficient. The one who solves problems before they start, keeps everything running smoothly, and rarely asks for help because needing others can feel dangerous.

- The Shadow: the part of your soul who mediates between your pain and your need for relief. The one who carries the feelings you think you're not supposed to have—anger, envy, desire, shame—and who escapes, self-sabotages, numbs, or lashes out to cope.
- The Young One: the soft, beating center beneath all your adult armor. This is the childlike heart at the center of your soul who carries unguarded longing and tenderness, curiosity and playful innocence, wonder, and the capacity to be wounded—the one waiting to be seen, welcomed, and loved.

Each one represents a different place within your soul mountain—a different way you learned to adapt and survive. Healing begins when you learn to tend to this inner world with care. You stop rejecting, analyzing, shaming, or fixing, and instead learn to create space for secure connection.

Because here's the good news: Each of these parts of your soul carries a longing for love, safety, and belonging. And each one can be restored as you recognize their bids and return to God's loving presence.[1]

RECOGNIZE A BID FOR CONNECTION

Take a deep breath. Slowly turn your attention inward.

Notice what's stirring inside you right now. Maybe it's a flicker of worry, the sting of something someone said earlier in the day, or the echo of a reaction you wish you'd handled differently.

1. What I'm noticing is:

If criticism, judgment, or shame arise, take a breath and remind yourself that this isn't about fixing anything. It's about restoring connection within. These bids are coming from a *part of your soul*—a specific place within you that's asking to be noticed and cared for.

2. If this part of you had a name, a shape, or an image, what would it be? (It might be "the Worrier" or look like a storm cloud.)

3. As you stay connected to this place within, get curious. Imagine this part of you had a voice. What does this part of your soul want you to know?

   What does this part of you fear?

   What does this part of you need?

   What does this part of you long for?

Take your time with what you notice. You're not interrogating—you're listening, the way you might listen to a loved one who's been carrying something heavy for a long time.

Express appreciation for this part of you: *Thank you for letting me know how you feel. I see that you're trying to help me. You don't have to do this alone.*

RETURN TO LOVE

Now imagine God's loving presence with you and with this part of your soul. There's no rush, no pressure. Just a growing awareness.

As you take a few slow breaths, notice what stirs.

1. What's it like to sit with the possibility that God is here with you now—and does this part of you have any fears or hesitations about God's closeness?

2. What might this part of your soul want to say—to you, or to God?

Let these words of Scripture settle into your soul:

"You have searched me, Lord, and you know me. . . . You hem me in behind and before, and you lay your hand upon me" (Ps. 139:1, 5).

Healing doesn't come from forcing change. It comes from allowing Love to enter the very places where you once felt alone.

STEP 9

MEET THE CONTROLLER WHO WORKS TOO HARD

One of the first parts you may notice inside is your Inner Controller. This is the part of you that developed early on to protect you when love felt far away or trust felt fragile.

Your Inner Controller learned quickly that in order to stay connected, she had to *manage* something, whether it was emotions, expectations, outcomes, or other people's reactions. When safety felt unpredictable, she became the one who tried to hold everything together.

The Controller shows up with plans, strategies, and checklists. She works overtime to make sure nothing falls apart, that you don't get blindsided, and that you stay one step ahead of disconnection.

The Controller wears different clothes on different people. In fact, the roles you learned in your family of origin are often different expressions of this Controller part, an internalized voice that tells you how to manage connection and stay safe.

- The Golden Child within may still whisper, *I have to succeed or I'll lose love.*
- The Caretaker within may still insist, *I can't rest until everyone else is okay.*
- The Comedian within may reassure, *If I keep things light, no one will leave or get angry.*
- The Invisible One within may still retreat, *If I stay quiet, I won't get hurt.*

- The Scapegoat within may still believe, *I'll always be blamed, no matter what I do.*
- The Rebel within may still declare, *No one's going to control me again.*

Each version looks a little different, but they all share the same root: a deep longing to protect against the threat of disconnection. This part of you attempts to *control* the situation so you won't have to feel the pain of being unwanted, unseen, or left alone. It believes that if it can just manage everything—your emotions, other people's behaviors, even God's responses—you might finally feel safe.

Here's the good news: Your Controller is trying to help. She's doing what she learned to do long ago when you were young and love felt fragile. She's working to protect you. But her protection comes at a cost. Instead of resting in love, she's always hustling to earn it. Instead of learning to find and trust genuine safety, she's working to create the illusion of it.

The journey forward isn't about shaming her but about learning to see her clearly. You learn to recognize her bids for connection and to thank her for how she helped you survive. And then, you help her return to the security of a Love that doesn't have to be managed or earned.

RECOGNIZE YOUR INNER CONTROLLER

1. When you think about the role you most identified with in Step 6, how does it surface as an internalized voice, impulse, or pattern of behavior?

2. How do you notice your Controller showing up in your life today—at work, at home, or in relationships?

3. What messages does she whisper to you? Perhaps something like "you have to be perfect" or "don't show any weakness"—or something entirely your own.

4. What does your Controller fear would happen if she didn't play this role?

5. How has this part of your soul helped you? What has it cost you?

RETURN TO LOVE

Now bring to mind an early memory of when you relied on this strategy to stay safe.

1. Jot down what you notice. How old is this younger version of you? What was she doing? How was she trying to help?

2. Picture her face. Her posture. The emotion in her eyes. She was doing the very best she could with what she had. Write a note of appreciation to this younger version of your Inner Controller. Simply thank her for what she's carried, and remind her she is no longer alone.

Dear younger me,

3. Circle or highlight the statement of truth she most needs to hear—or write your own:

You are loved, even when you make mistakes.
You can speak up truthfully and still be safe.
You are not responsible for keeping everyone else together.
You don't have to impress anyone to be loved.
You are not bad, broken, or to blame for what went wrong.
You are loved even when you're not "okay."

If it's helpful, imagine God's steady presence drawing near to this younger version of yourself. You might whisper a simple prayer over her:

God, thank you for the part of me that worked so hard to protect me. Teach her to rest. Teach me to trust. And help us both lean into your love, where we are already safe.

STEP 10

TEACH THE CONTROLLER TO REST

By now, you've begun to recognize your Inner Controller. You've noticed how she works overtime to keep you safe by perfecting, overfunctioning, or staying hyperalert. You've traced some of her roots back to childhood, when taking responsibility for others felt like the only way to keep connection from slipping away.

In many ways, the Controller acts like the parent of your inner world. She behaves as if she's the one responsible for holding everything together. Sometimes she even tries to "play God," convinced it's her job to keep you safe. She whispers, *If I don't handle this, no one will. If I don't get this right, everything will fall apart.*

Your Inner Controller may struggle to rest or step back, because she learned early on that no one else would carry the weight with her. At her core, she finds it hard to let go—not only when it comes to trusting that other people might show up for her, but even more so when it comes to trusting that God will.

She often maps onto God the disappointments and attachment wounds left by caregivers who did not show up in the ways she needed, who didn't provide love, guidance, support, or healthy boundaries. And so she operates in a silo within your soul, holding all the threads together, even as she feels utterly alone and exhausted.

But the truth is, she was never meant to carry this much responsibility. Her vigilance may have been necessary once, but it isn't the way to wholeness now.

One of my favorite biblical pictures of the Controller appears in the story of Martha and Mary in Luke 10. Martha was busy, bustling, managing the details, frustrated that Mary wasn't helping. Mary, on the other hand, sat quietly at Jesus' feet.

I recognize both Mary and Martha parts within my own soul. But the Martha part of me completely understands what may have been driving her in that moment:

If I don't get this done, no one will. (teeth clenched)

Mary always leaves everything up to me! (exasperated)

Notice what Jesus said as he addressed her Inner Controller. He didn't scold Martha. He recognized her anxiety:

"Martha, Martha . . . you are worried and upset about many things, but few things are needed—or indeed only one" (Luke 10:41–42).

Her Inner Controller was working hard to hold everything together, but she was missing the one thing she needed most: *presence.*

If she could have paused to recognize the anxious, overfunctioning part of herself, she might have taken a deep breath, set down the dishes, and sat at the feet of Jesus, alongside Mary. There she would have received his nourishment and rest, and then returned to her daily tasks from a far more grounded, peaceful place. Instead of working from a place of pressure, she'd be working from a place of love.

The invitation isn't to banish your Controller. She is part of you. She will always want to help. The invitation is to help her release her burden of being solely responsible and to share the weight she was never meant to carry alone.

As your Controller learns to trust that Love is holding what she once had to manage alone, her role begins to change. She doesn't disappear—she transforms.

She becomes your inner Steward. A Steward still cares. She still takes responsibility. But she no longer operates from fear or urgency. She acts from presence, discernment, and trust. Instead of trying to control outcomes, she carefully tends what has been entrusted to her.

It can be hard to trust that safety is possible, even for a moment. But change starts as you begin to *recognize* when your Inner Controller is starting to take over. Each recognition is a pause, a doorway back into connection.

RECOGNIZE YOUR PATTERNS OF CONTROL

1. What are the signals that you're grasping for control? For example:

   - *I'm frantically working instead of enjoying this time with my family, my friends, or my guests.*
   - *I'm pretending as if I'm fine, when in truth, I'm hurting.*
   - *I'm stepping in to redirect this conversation, even though it's not my job to manage their conflict.*

2. When you think of Martha and Mary, how does your Controller view each person in the story? Mary? Martha? Jesus?

3. How does your Inner Controller imagine God? For example:

   - *Distant: God is far away. I can't count on him, so I hold it all together myself.*
   - *Demanding: God expects me to get it right, or he'll be disappointed.*
   - *Critical: God is watching for my mistakes. I can't rest or let my guard down.*
   - *Unpredictable: Sometimes God feels close, but other times he disappears. I never know if he'll come through.*

4. Now imagine a God who is present—not demanding more from you but inviting you to rest in his care. What does your Inner Controller most need—from you, or from God?

5. What gentle invitation might God be offering your Controller today?

RETURN TO LOVE

Picture your Controller. Maybe she's at her laptop, checking her to-do list, smoothing over a conversation, or standing guard with arms crossed.

Let her know you're with her. You might say:

- *I'm here now.*
- *Thank you for working so hard to keep me safe.*
- *I see how tired you are.*

1. How does she respond to your presence?

2. Now imagine God drawing near. How does this part of you respond to God's presence?

3. What does this part of your soul need—from you, or from God?

Take a moment and say a prayer on behalf of your hardworking Inner Controller. Just as you might intercede for a child you love, you can also intercede for a part of yourself.

God, thank you for loving my Inner Controller—the one who works so hard to keep me safe. Thank you for her diligence and care. Please show this part of me that she doesn't have to manage everything alone. Help her trust that she is safe in your presence.

Genuine connectedness isn't built through control. It's built through presence.

STEP 11

DISCOVER THE SHADOW WHO HIDES YOUR HURT

The Shadow is the part of you that mediates between pain and your need for relief. Unlike the Controller, she doesn't usually show up polished, pleasing, or on alert. Instead, she tends to linger at the edges of your soul, moving in ways that are shadowy, impulsive, or reactive, often before you even realize she's there.

You might catch a glimpse of her in the sharp words you say (or think) and wish you could take back, in the midnight snack you didn't even want, or in the endless scroll that keeps you up long past bedtime. She lingers in unspoken resentments, comparison, and envy. She's the part of you that gives voice to what is painful, messy, unfiltered, and raw.

Most of us have been taught that our Shadow is the enemy. If we could just do better, be more disciplined, or surrender more, this part of us would go away. But I want you to consider a different strategy.

What if this part of you *also* needs secure connection?

The Shadow often feels like the inner enemy within your soul, the part of you that carries shame and blame, the one you wish you could make go away.

For years I lived with a part of me that could shred my soul with cruel words. I called her my inner eviscerator. She beat me down internally long before anyone else ever could. I tried to bury this part of me. I begged God to take her away. I tried to outrun her.

But the more I rejected her, the louder she became.

Then Jesus' words in Matthew 5:44 stopped me in my tracks: "Love your enemies. Let them bring out the best in you, not the worst" (MSG).

And it hit me: Jesus wasn't only talking about *external* enemies. He was also speaking to the enemies within—the parts we demonize, dislike, and try to destroy.[1]

Over time, I learned to recognize this Inner Shadow. I learned to see her not as an enemy but as a part of me who needed care, to get curious about her story, and to *connect* with her. I learned about her isolation, her fear, and her experiences of rejection, and how she was trying to help me survive by *hurting me before others could.*

And slowly, something astonishing happened. The more I connected with her—without judgment, shame, or criticism—the more she softened.

The more she learned to trust me. And the more she opened up her heart to God.

The very one who once tore me apart has become my most trusted Inner Seer, the one who encourages, illuminates truth, and helps me be brave.

Your Shadow might lash out, manipulate, disappear, or self-sabotage. For example, you might notice that you:

- Snap at your spouse when you really feel lonely
- Criticize a coworker when you actually feel insecure
- Shop, scroll, or binge when you feel sad or scared or alone
- Shut down when a friend gets too close

Shame whispers: *You're bad. You're unlovable. You'll never change.*

But shame never heals. It only drives the Shadow deeper underground.

Jesus shows us a different way. After Peter denied him, Jesus didn't heap on shame. Instead, he restored him: "Do you love me? . . . Feed my sheep" (John 21:15–17). He named the wound, acknowledged the failure, and gave Peter new purpose. That's how Shadows are healed—not through condemnation but through connection.

Here's the truth: Your Shadow is not your enemy. She's wounded. She's weary. And she's crying out for your attention. She doesn't need your contempt—she's had enough of that. She needs your compassion and your help to return to Love, heal, and become your Inner Seer.

RECOGNIZE YOUR INNER SHADOW

1. As a child, when love or trust felt uncertain, how did you manage pain (lashed out, withdrew, numbed, criticized yourself or someone else, etc.)?

2. What is an early memory of when this part of you picked up this strategy?

3. How do you notice your Shadow showing up in your life today?

4. What messages does she whisper to you? Perhaps something like "See? This is why nothing ever works out" or "They don't get to hurt you and walk away"—or something entirely your own.

5. What does your Shadow fear will happen if she doesn't do her job?

6. How has this part of your soul helped you? What has it cost you?

Your Shadow's outbursts aren't random. They are signals—clumsy, often messy attempts to let you know that you've stumbled onto an old wound or a tender place within your soul. What if, instead of condemning her, you could learn to recognize her cues and help her learn another way to cope, heal, and grow?

RETURN TO LOVE

Bring to mind an early memory of when you first learned to cope in a less-than-healthy way—when pain felt too big, and this strategy helped you feel some relief or protection.

1. Jot down what you notice. How old is this younger version of you? What was she doing? How was she trying to help?

If you notice shame or discomfort surface, that's okay. Acknowledge those feelings too. Remember that this work isn't about forcing closeness. It's about creating safety. Move at your own pace, and seek support if you need it.

2. Write a note of appreciation to this younger version of you, the one trying to cope with pain. You might thank her for how she stepped in when pain felt too big, for the relief she was trying to offer, or remind her she is no longer alone.

Dear younger me,

Now, if it's helpful, imagine God's compassionate presence drawing near to that place in you, without judgment or shame.

3. What my Shadow needs most from me is:

4. What my Shadow needs most from God is:

If it's helpful, whisper a simple prayer over her:

God, help me see my Shadow not as my enemy but as a part of me who needs care. Thank you for loving me in the middle of my darkest moments. Teach me to meet this part of myself with your loving presence, wise containment, and compassion.

That's how Shadows are healed—not through condemnation but through the slow work of establishing secure connection.

STEP 12

HEAL THE SHADOW'S STORY

The Shadow isn't meant to be destroyed. It's meant to be transformed. The very impulses that once drove you into hiding, lashing out, or numbing can, when met with compassion and God's presence, become surprising gifts.

The Shadow part of you is often passionate, creative, and deeply feeling. These aren't flaws—not at all! They are beautiful qualities that can get tangled up with pain. When these qualities aren't cared for, they can lead to the Shadow acting out. But when shame is replaced with kindness and fear is replaced with safety, the Shadow becomes a trusted inner friend. She turns her sensitivity toward truth-telling, her hunger toward God, and her fire toward protecting what is good and right and true.

Here are a few common Shadow behaviors, and how they often transform when met with compassion and God's presence:

- **RESENTMENT → RIGHTEOUS DISCERNMENT.** Resentment often signals that a boundary has been crossed or a need has been ignored. Transformed, it becomes clear-eyed discernment and the courage to advocate for healthy patterns with honesty and grace.
- **ENVY → VISION AND CALLING.** Envy reveals longings you may have buried or dismissed. Transformed, it becomes clarity about your true desires and the courage to pursue your God-given talents.
- **LASHING OUT → COURAGEOUS ACTION.** Lashing out is often a frantic attempt to escape discomfort or loneliness and shift blame. Transformed, it becomes brave, creative action aligned with your deepest values.

- **NUMBING → DEEP REST AND RENEWAL.** Numbing tries to protect you from overwhelm or pain. Transformed, it becomes wisdom about when your soul needs rest, comfort, or renewal.
- **CONTEMPT TOWARD SELF OR OTHERS → INSIGHT AND TRUTH-TELLING.** Harsh criticism is often rooted in fear and old shame. Transformed, it becomes the gift of insight—naming truth in ways that heal rather than harm.
- **FANTASY → IMAGINATION AND HEALING.** Fantasy offers temporary escape through daydreams, idealized scenarios, or stories that help you avoid what hurts. Transformed, it becomes sacred imagination: a creative space where you can process pain, envision new possibilities, and allow God to meet you with hope, beauty, and healing.

Mary Magdalene is one of the most powerful examples of a redeemed Shadow from the Bible. Scripture tells us she was tormented by seven demons (Luke 8:2), a life marked by chaos, rejection, and profound inner torment. In many ways, Mary embodies what it means to live out of the Shadow: to be misunderstood, isolated, and plagued by wounds others could not see.

But when she encountered Jesus, everything changed. He did not shame her. He *saw* her. He *restored* her. And that same intensity of spirit that once left her tormented became the very strength that enabled her to stay when others fled. Mary remained near the cross as Jesus died (John 19:25). And she was the first to witness and proclaim his resurrection (John 20:16–18).

Mary's Shadow wasn't erased—it was redeemed. Her deep longing, once twisted by torment, became a fierce devotion and a prophetic voice. Through staying connected with Jesus, the part of her that once drove her into the dark became the very part that carried the light of resurrection.

RECOGNIZE THE MOVEMENTS OF YOUR SHADOW

Think back to a recent time when you acted out in a way you didn't like (big or small).

1. What was the triggering event that set it off?

2. What did you do (lashed out, withdrew, numbed, self-criticized, vented, etc.)?

3. How was your Shadow trying to help you?

4. Consider the list of transformed Shadow behaviors. What deeper invitation might be presenting itself to your Shadow?

Naming the pain—and the invitation—is the beginning of transformation. Your Shadow is not the enemy. She's sending you a signal about where healing is needed and where new life wants to grow.

RETURN TO LOVE

Use the chart below to help you honor the pain behind the Shadow's feelings. In the left column, write the messages you tell yourself when your Shadow shows up. In the right column, write what your wisest self, God, or a loving parent might say in response.

Here are a few examples to get you started:

- *Shame: People always leave. I'm not worth staying. | Compassion: I am with you. I will not leave you.*
- *Shame: I'm a failure. I'll never get it right. | Compassion: You are not finished yet. You are dearly beloved.*
- *Shame: I always overreact. I'm too much. | Compassion: I see how much you care. I can hold it with you.*

Shame's Voice	**Compassion's Voice**
1.	1.
2.	2.
3.	3.
4.	4.

Choose one message from the first column (Shame's Voice) that feels most familiar to you right now. Say it aloud, allowing yourself to hear the raw honesty of the words. Notice what feelings rise up in your body.

Next, pause and take a deep breath. Imagine God's steady presence with you, right there in the ache. Then, read the corresponding response from the second column (Compassion's Voice) slowly, as if you were speaking it directly to this part of you.

1. What do you notice—in your body? In your soul?

2. If it feels helpful, imagine the Shadow part of you standing near the empty tomb with Mary Magdalene. Jesus calls her by name. She is seen. She is loved. What do you notice?

Your goal in this exercise is to acknowledge the pain beneath your Shadow without excusing the actions she took—or might be tempted to take. With God's help, you are learning to become a wise inner parent to yourself, honoring the legitimacy of your pain while guiding this Shadow part of your soul into transformation through steady, loving presence.

STEP 13

RECLAIM THE YOUNG ONE INSIDE YOU

As the noise of the Controller and the Shadow begins to soften, you'll become aware of a quieter voice beneath them. This one is a tender presence, one that's marked by innocence, play, and wonder.

This is the Young One inside you.

Often, she shows up indirectly, through moments of tenderness, sudden vulnerability, a longing to be seen, or an ache you can't quite explain. Sometimes she appears as a desire to be rescued. Other times, you'll sense her through a pull toward beauty, play, or curiosity.

The Young One is the part of you that experiences connection most directly. When she feels unseen or alone, the Controller and Shadow rush in to manage the pain, through control, distraction, or withdrawal. That's why tending to the Young One isn't indulgent or regressive. It's foundational. She carries your earliest imprint of love, and she remembers what it was like when love felt absent or out of reach. When she begins to feel safe, the rest of your inner world can settle.

Scripture offers a beautiful picture of this kind of inner safety. The psalmist writes, "I have calmed and quieted my soul, like a weaned child with [its] mother; like a weaned child is my soul within me" (Ps. 131:2 NKJV).

This image isn't one of helplessness or dependence but of *settled trust.* A weaned child no longer clings in panic or cries out in fear. She rests because she is held, known, and secure in the presence of someone who can be trusted. This is the posture of the Young One inside your soul when safety begins to return. Not striving. Not hiding. Simply being—held within the care of Love.

The Young One isn't weak. She's not a problem to fix. She's the tender center beneath your adult armor, the place where both ache and wisdom live.

When she's tended with care, the Controller doesn't have to work so hard, and the Shadow doesn't have to reach for escape. Your inner world steadies from the center all the way out.

RECOGNIZE THE YOUNG ONE

Over the next few days, notice moments when you feel:

- *unexpectedly small or tender*
- *deeply moved by something beautiful*
- *unusually sensitive to rejection or exclusion*
- *a longing to be cared for, reassured, or held*
- *an urge to rescue someone else*
- *a spontaneous impulse toward play (laughing, exploring, or doing something just because it's fun)*

These are often signals of the Young One's presence.

When you notice one of these moments, pause and ask yourself: Something tender is here. Can I stay present with it, without fixing or silencing it?

Notice what feelings surface. If they start to feel too big to hold alone, that's a sign to slow down—not to push through. You might place a hand on your heart, take a few steady breaths, or step away and return later. Sometimes the Young One carries big feelings, especially as you first start to connect with her.

If it feels helpful, reach for support. You could say to someone you trust, "I'm feeling tender right now, and I'm not sure why. Can you stay with me for a few minutes?" Or you can simply journal what you notice, without trying to figure it all out.

This work isn't about forcing access. It's about creating safety.

Take a moment to note anything you've noticed.

RETURN TO LOVE

This week, practice offering the Young One care through intentional, concrete actions.

Choose one small act that nurtures wonder, safety, or delight. Set aside time to prioritize this activity, staying mindful of how it feels to the Young One inside you. Here are some examples:

- *spending time in nature*
- *listening to music*
- *dancing or moving your body*
- *playing or creating*
- *resting or relaxing without productivity*

In her beautiful book *The Artist's Way*, Julia Cameron describes something similar and calls it an "Artist Date"—a small, intentional time set aside to nourish the creative, childlike part of you.[1] You can think of this practice in the same way. It's not about self-improvement but a practice of presence. You're offering the Young One your attention, not asking her to perform or explain herself.

After this time with the Young One, take a moment to reflect. What was it like to be with her?

Nurturing your wonder, curiosity, and sense of play, while staying mindful of the Young One, is one of the ways you restore safe connection.

Next, if you'd like, read this story slowly:

> The people brought children to Jesus, hoping he might touch them. The disciples shooed them off. But Jesus was irate and let them know it: "Don't push these children away. Don't ever get between them and me. These children are at the very center of life in the kingdom. Mark this: Unless you accept God's kingdom in the simplicity of a child, you'll never get in." Then, gathering the children up in his arms, he laid his hands of blessing on them.
> (Mark 10:13–16 MSG)

Now imagine yourself as the young child in this scene.

1. What does it feel like to hear other adults shooing you away?

2. What does it feel like to hear Jesus rebuke those same adults, call you in close, and gather you into his arms?

Picture how God sees this Young One: beloved, precious, wonderfully made, full of dignity, full of possibility. While other voices may have told her to stay quiet, be strong, or to hide her needs, Jesus responds to this Young One with *delight,* whispering, *Come. You belong with me.*

Healing doesn't begin with effort but with welcome.

STEP 14

TEND YOUR DEEPEST LONGING

You've begun to recognize the presence of the Young One inside you, not as a problem to fix but as a tender, childlike part of you. Now, we'll move one layer deeper. Instead of focusing on who she is, you'll explore what she needs most.

Every person—every soul—carries a handful of foundational needs. These needs aren't childish. They're the building blocks of your soul, and they live on in your nervous system long after childhood ends. When these needs go unmet early in life, they leave an ache.

As adults, we often misinterpret the ache of the Young One as insecurity, being "too sensitive," "too much," or overreacting. But at its root, the ache is simply a younger part of you, saying:

Please see me.

Please keep me safe.

Please don't leave me behind.

When you begin to recognize this ache, you learn more about your soul's core needs, the ones that may never have gotten met and the ones that were met and yet still remain, simply because you're human. The Young One inside no longer feels like a burden. She becomes a guide, showing you where connection or care is needed and where God wants to draw near.

Here are the six common longings of the Young One. Each of these needs is universal. Some were met better than others. What changes from person to person is which one aches the loudest in adulthood.

1. THE NEED TO BE *SEEN*

CHILDHOOD ROOT: Subtle hurts—your raised hand that never got called on, the heartbreak that went unnoticed, the talent no one named—become early lessons in invisibility.

ADULT FORM: The Shadow may quietly seek attention, while the Controller over-achieves so no one can overlook you again. The Young One just needed someone to look at her and say, *I see you*.

2. THE NEED FOR *SAFETY*

CHILDHOOD ROOT: Unpredictable moods, inconsistent care, or a caregiver who simply wasn't available taught you that comfort and support are not guaranteed.

ADULT FORM: The Controller tries to outrun uncertainty while the Shadow deflects fear into distrust of others or self-blame. The Young One within you needed someone to soothe her when she felt afraid.

3. THE NEED TO *BELONG*

CHILDHOOD ROOT: Being left out, not being picked, or sensing another child was the "favorite" created early impressions of scarcity.

ADULT FORM: The Controller constantly scans for cues as a way to gauge where she stands. The Shadow's flicker of relief when someone else falters isn't malice but often grief. The Young One needed someone to help her find her own sense of place.

4. THE NEED FOR *WORTH*

CHILDHOOD ROOT: When praise only followed achievement, or affection seemed conditional, you internalized the belief that worth must be earned (or proven).

ADULT FORM: The Controller perfects and performs, while the Shadow collapses when perfection falters. The Young One needed to experience the truth of her inherent belovedness.

5. THE NEED TO *FEEL*

CHILDHOOD ROOT: If feelings were minimized (*Others have it worse*), mocked, or punished (*Stop crying!*), you may have learned to hide your inner world.

ADULT FORM: Emotion becomes either reactive (via the Shadow) or suppressed (via the Controller). The Young One simply needed someone to help her learn to identify her feelings and regulate them in healthy ways.

6. THE NEED TO BE *HELD*

CHILDHOOD ROOT: When you were overwhelmed—emotionally, physically, or relationally—and no one came close, or comfort came with conditions, you learned that your pain was too much to bring to another person.

ADULT FORM: The Controller manages distress alone and never asks for help, while the Shadow escapes when pain becomes too great. The Young One needed someone to draw close, hold the weight with her, and stay.

Each of these six needs—being seen, being safe, belonging, knowing your worth, having permission to feel, and being held—form the emotional landscape of the Young One inside you.

When these needs go unmet, they don't disappear; they simply shift underground, embedded deep within the contours of your soul, waiting for a safer time to surface. That's why adult reactions can feel so outsized or confusing, because they're rooted in long-ago moments when you had to make sense of a world on your own.

As you begin to identify which need surfaces most in you today, you're simply making room. You're creating the space this younger part of you *always* needed, the space where healing begins and where God meets you with tenderness, not shame.

RECOGNIZE YOUR DEEPEST LONGING

Think of a recent moment when you felt small, tender, or overly reactive.

1. What happened?

2. What do you notice stirring in your body? In your soul?

3. How did you protect yourself in that moment?

4. What did the Young One inside most need? *(Circle as many as apply or write your own.)*

- *To be seen*
- *To feel safe*
- *To belong*
- *To know her worth*
- *To let her feelings come out*
- *To be held*

5. If you could put that need into one simple request, what might it be?

This is how you begin to recognize the bids from the Young One. It may be that what she needs most is *you.*

RETURN TO LOVE

Stay with the moment you just named. Now imagine yourself with this younger version of you. Or you might imagine what your wisest, gentlest self would say to a beloved child or dear friend who felt this way.

If you feel anything other than tenderness or compassion—maybe frustration, irritation, embarrassment, or distance—notice those responses with curiosity. They might be coming from your Inner Controller or your Shadow, or they might be echoes of old messages you absorbed from others.

1. How does she respond to compassion?

If it's helpful, picture God turning toward this Young One with warmth and steady kindness. He bends down to her height. He calls her by name. He gathers her close, simply because she belongs to him.

2. How does she respond to God's presence?

3. What does she most need from you or from God in this moment?

Write a brief prayer, just a few simple lines. Or you can borrow this one:

God, stay near this Young One who still feels small and tender. Help her sense her belovedness. Teach me how to care for her with your help, with patience, gentleness, and love.

Healing begins when no part of your soul has to hide any longer, when every part of you comes home to Love.

STEP 15

WELCOME EVERY PART HOME TO LOVE

Imagine a feast at the center of your soul, a long, welcoming table. One by one, the parts of your soul find their seats. The Controller takes a deep breath as she settles in, her shoulders softening as she realizes she can release her grip. The Shadow steps out from the corners, no longer hiding, no longer bracing—just taking her place with quiet dignity. And the Young One—the tender, most vulnerable part of you—comes forward to the seat of honor, right next to God at the center.

When you welcome these parts of your soul with compassion, you can begin to reparent them, offering the presence, care, and safety they still need. And when all of this unfolds within the steadiness of God's presence, something beautiful begins to take shape.

Your soul starts to emanate love, peace, and joy—quiet, steady, growing. The kind of inner confidence and security that doesn't have to strive or hide. The kind of wholeness that grows from the inside out.

Your Controller no longer has to strain to hold everything together. Instead, she becomes a steady, capable steward: wise, grounded, and clear.

Your Shadow no longer tries to slip away or disappear. Instead, she becomes a discerning Seer, offering honesty, insight, and courage.

And the Young One no longer feels lonely, invisible, or sidelined. Instead, she finally feels free, held by the truth of her belovedness. She moves with ease and delight, secure in God's love.

With God's presence anchoring the table, every part of you can finally rest in the larger harmony. This is how wholeness begins: when each part of your soul knows it belongs, and you learn to live connected—always—to Love.

RECOGNIZE THE TABLE OF LOVE IN YOUR SOUL

Imagine your inner soul as a table, a place of welcome, warmth, and belonging, where each part of you is invited to gather.

Now, one by one, picture each part of your soul arriving. Pause after each one to reflect and write what you notice below.

Picture your Controller arriving, shoulders tense, scanning the room, unsure what will be asked of her.

1. What does your Controller need to feel welcomed?

2. Picture your Shadow lingering at the edge, unsure, hesitant, maybe tempted to turn away. What does your Shadow need to feel welcomed?

3. Finally, picture the Young One also being welcomed—your tender, childlike self. Notice how Jesus meets her and gathers her in his arms, calling her "beloved."

4. What does the Young One need to feel welcomed?

5. Take a moment to find or draw an image that represents a feast or welcoming table, a picture that captures what your own soul feels like when every part of you is gathered in love.

RETURN TO LOVE

Now imagine Jesus at the center of the table, welcoming your soul with love. Notice what shifts as each part realizes it belongs—not in competition with the others but together, and with God.

1. Take a moment to notice two things for each part of you—a burden and a longing. What burden is each part of you ready to release? What does each part of you long to receive?

   Controller:

Shadow:

Young One:

2. What shifts inside your soul as you consider both your burdens and your longings?

Here is a prayer I return to often, one that helps me welcome each part of my soul into the presence of God. Feel free to borrow these words or let them spark a prayer of your own.

Jesus, I'm here. And you are here, too, closer than breath. Not only God above but Christ with me.

Christ with me when I grasp or clutch.
Christ with me when I want to hide or flee.
Christ with me when I feel most tender.
Christ with me when I long to be seen.
Hold every part of me until my soul remembers—always—what it feels like to return to Love.

PART TWO

LOVE NOTES TO SECURE YOUR SOUL

You've spent the first part of this companion guide learning to ground yourself. You've looked at the patterns that have shaped your soul, noticed the parts of you that work so hard within, and opened these tender places to your own awareness and to the steady presence of God's love. Part One has been the root system—a slow, deepening journey of awareness and connection.

Now you're ready for something a little different.

Part Two is designed to meet you in real life, in the moments when trust feels fragile, old fears resurface, or your footing feels unsteady. It's organized around the six qualities we explored in *The Secure Soul*:

1. Secure Your Soul in God's Love
2. Secure Your Sense of Worth
3. Secure Your Soul Through Inner Repair
4. Secure Your Soul Through Risk
5. Secure Your Soul Through Transition
6. Secure Your Soul in Relationships

Think of the pages ahead as a collection of soul-sized reminders. You don't need to read them in order. Instead, turn to the section that feels most resonant in this season or in this moment.

As you read, make each note your own. Add the details that fit your story, including your fears, your patterns of protection, and the truths that bring your soul a sense of calm. You might imagine each love note coming from the wisest part of yourself or from the loving God who knows your story and holds it with care. If it helps, you can also read them as if they are coming from me, or from any voice you trust.

Here's what to expect: Each subsection starts with a brief overview of a particular quality of a secure soul. You'll then find several Love Notes to Your Soul, shaped by the most common questions and struggles I hear in my work. Each Love Note includes A Pause for the Soul. This is a space to slow down, respond in writing, and notice what stirs within you. At the end of each section, you'll find a Going Deeper exercise to help you integrate what you're learning into your inner life and daily rhythms.

This is the sacred work of rewriting the old messages of disconnection with new ones rooted in presence, compassion, and truth—one love note to your soul at a time.

SECURE YOUR SOUL IN GOD'S LOVE

A secure soul is rooted in loving connection—not in your performance, not in your spiritual enthusiasm, not in how well you pray or how strong your faith feels on any given day. A secure soul rests inside the steady, unchanging presence of God, who is always with you. It knows—deep in your body and soul, not just in your head—that Love holds firm even when your emotions fluctuate, even when parts of you panic, shut down, or go silent.

But for many of us, this kind of security doesn't come naturally.

You might *believe* God is loving yet still *feel* disconnected, afraid, ashamed, or overwhelmed.

You might long for closeness with God but experience only distance or confusion.

And while your mind tries to reason its way back to trust, your nervous system replays its oldest wiring, patterns shaped long before you ever formed beliefs about God.

This is not a failure of faith.

It's the language of *attachment*.

A secure base in God's love begins when you stop trying to "feel spiritual" and start gently tending to *inner bids for connection*. You begin to notice when your Controller tries too hard, when your Shadow feels shame, or when the Young One aches for belonging.

As you recognize each bid for connection and return to God's loving presence right there, you learn to secure your soul through *every* circumstance.

WHEN GOD FEELS FAR AWAY

Dear one,

There are moments when God feels impossibly far away—when prayer feels like talking into the void, when Scripture feels flat, when worship leaves you disconnected.

Sometimes you even feel afraid to admit it: *I believe in God . . . so why don't I sense God's loving presence?*

I want you to know this: *Feeling* disconnected from God does not mean you *are* disconnected from God.

For reasons we don't always understand, God sometimes feels far away. You cry out, but the heavens seem quiet. That ache is real, and it can feel unbearable. Please know it's not your fault. Don't let anyone blame you for those times in life when God feels far away, even when you're reaching out.

When you face this kind of distance, remember *even then* you're not alone. Wonderful luminaries of the faith have felt far from God at times throughout history. St. John of the Cross called it the dark night of the soul.[1] Even Jesus felt forsaken by God, crying out "My God, my God, why have you forsaken me?" (Matt. 27:46).

Silence doesn't mean abandonment, nor does it mean you've fallen out of relationship.

God's love holds steady, even when you can't feel it.

This ache you feel—the longing, the confusion, the distance—isn't a sign of spiritual failure. It's evidence of a soul that's intact, that a part of you is *longing for closeness*. Your work is to stay with your soul right there, *in that place of longing.*

Sometimes, even in seasons when God feels far away, your soul still recognizes love in unexpected ways. It might be when you are with someone safe, when you're in nature, when music moves you, or when you're absorbed in something that brings a sense of peace or aliveness.

These moments matter. They point you to God's presence. Scripture says, "Every good and perfect gift is from above, coming down from the Father of the heavenly lights" (James 1:17). Every place you encounter goodness or safety and every moment your soul comes alive to hope or possibility, you are touching something that originates in God.

When you return to these moments with intention, you strengthen the neural pathways in your brain that recognize safety and loving presence, pathways you may never have been taught to trust.

You don't have to fight the disconnection.

Just stay honest.

Just stay open.

Just keep breathing.

Love is already on the way.

With you always,

♡

A PAUSE FOR THE SOUL

If God feels distant, take a deep breath and notice the stirrings within your soul.[2]

A part of me feels:

When I picture this part of me, I see:

The fears/doubts/longings rising in me are:

Another time I felt this way was (recent or long ago):

What was happening then was:

The message I learned or assumed was:

The moments when I feel most held or connected are:

What my soul needs from me is:

What I long to hear from God is:

Notice whatever shows up with compassion and curiosity. Don't try to fix, preach, or convince. Simply be with the part of you as she shares her experience with you.

WHEN IT'S HARD TO PRAY

Dear one,

You want to connect with God, but the words or focus won't come. Your mind drifts or your heart feels closed. You're finding it hard to pray. You feel distracted, distant, or maybe even fearful.

But let me remind you:

Prayer doesn't begin with your effort. Prayer begins with God's presence.

Your soul aches for God's loving presence, but sometimes parts of you don't know how to let that presence in.

Sometimes a part of you is distracted. Life pulls you in a thousand directions. Your Inner Controller takes over. She's trying to help, but she keeps the lists running, the deadlines looming, and whispers, *There's no time to stop.*

Sometimes a part of you is fearful. You're carrying a secret, a burden, or a wound. The Shadow part of you wants to hide, self-soothe, or numb, fearful of risking God's anger or rejection. She whispers, *It's easier not to try. God doesn't want to bother with you.*

And sometimes prayer is hard because life has been heavy. Your body is tired, and your emotions are simply worn thin. Connection requires vulnerability, and the exhausted or overwhelmed part of you has closed the door.

Here's the beautiful paradox: Often, the very part of you that keeps you from prayer *is the place in your soul most in need of it.*

You don't have to push harder.

You don't have to produce the "right" feelings.

You don't have to "fix" yourself to pray.

All you need to do is stay connected to whatever part of you is showing up right now.

I see that you're reluctant to pray.

I see that your worry, exhaustion, or fear is getting in the way.

It's okay.

I'm here with you.

And God is here too.

Simply speak what's true.

Stay present to whatever part of you is most real.

Because this is where God's presence *has already found you.*

Dear one, when you *stay with your own soul*—no matter how fearful, distracted, or hesitant—you remind yourself what connection feels like. Your breath slows. Your body softens.

As Brother Lawrence so beautifully said, you are *practicing the presence of God*—even here.[1]

With you always,

♡

A PAUSE FOR THE SOUL

If prayer feels hard, take a deep breath and notice the stirrings within your soul.

I find it hardest to pray when:

A part of me feels:

When I picture this part of me, I see:

Another time I felt this way was (recent or long ago):

What was happening then was:

When prayer feels hard, the message I tell myself is:

What this part of my soul needs from me is:

What this part of my soul longs to hear from God is:

Stay present to whatever shows up. Don't try to force a specific response. Simply be with the part of you as she shares her experience with you.

WHEN YOU FEEL LIKE CHECKING OUT

Dear one,

I know how it feels when your soul is tired: when you feel overloaded, when you're overwhelmed, and when even the smallest spiritual practices feel out of reach.

When you're stretched thin, everything feels harder: prayer, connection, trust, even simple presence.

In moments like this, different parts of you react in different ways. Your Controller pressures you to keep moving, to hold it together, or to try harder. Your Shadow tempts you to numb out, shut down, or avoid. And all the while, the Young One inside feels discouraged, defeated, or forgotten.

When you feel like checking out, it's easy to blame yourself. But the truth is often more tender: An urge to check out is usually a sign that something in you is weary.

Weariness isn't failure. It's a bid for connection—your soul asking for care.

Sometimes your soul is tired because life has been heavy, because you've held too much for too long. And sometimes it's weary because you need some space to breathe, to recharge, to play, or simply to be.

Recognizing the pull to check out with compassion isn't indulgence; it's wisdom.

You're not pushing. You're *listening.*

You're tending to what is real inside you.

Dear one, this weary part of your soul isn't a problem to be solved. It's a beloved place to be tended. This weariness isn't a sign of spiritual inadequacy. It's an invitation to *move at the pace of compassion.*

And you can trust this: God meets you most gently in these places where strength runs thin. God's presence doesn't arrive with pressure, but with the gentle nearness of one who knows—and loves—this part of your soul, even in its weakness.

You are allowed to rest.

You are allowed to be held.

You are allowed to let Love come to you, slowly, in this very place.

With you always,

♡

A PAUSE FOR THE SOUL

If you feel like checking out, take a deep breath and notice the stirrings within.
A part of me feels:

When I picture this part of me, I see:

The fears/doubts/longings rising in me are:

Another time I felt this way was (recent or long ago):

What was happening then was:

The message I learned or assumed was:

What this part of me is longing for is:

Now imagine this weary part of you—small, curled up, overwhelmed—sitting beside you. Then imagine how you might care for a beloved child or friend who felt this way.

How I can care for this part of me right now is:

Imagine God drawing near—not asking anything of you, not demanding effort, not requiring enthusiasm—just offering presence.

What this part of me longs to hear from God is:

Take a slow breath and stay present. Don't try to pressure yourself. Simply be with the part of you as she shares her experience with you.

GOING DEEPER: MEET GOD ON THE MOUNTAIN[1]

This practice is drawn from chapter 8 of *The Secure Soul*. It's a gentle way to notice how your inner world responds to God's presence.

You can read this reflection slowly on your own or listen to the guided audio using the QR code at the end of this exercise. There's no one right way to imagine your inner world—just an invitation.

If you're reading this on the page, consider reading it through once without stopping. Then read it a second time slowly, pausing to jot a few words or notes when something stands out.

Take a moment to settle into your body. Close your eyes if you'd like, and take a few slow, steady breaths.

Now imagine your inner world as a mountain landscape. Not a mountain you must climb to prove something. But a mountain that represents your soul.

There may be wooded areas. Rocky places. Open meadows. Shaded valleys.

You are standing within its hills.

As you take in the terrain, pause and notice: Who is here with you?

You may sense different parts of your soul—perhaps a vigilant one scanning for danger, a weary one sitting nearby, or a fearful one holding your hand.

Take a moment to note a word or two about the different parts of you who are present:

Now imagine inviting each of these parts of you to take a walk with you. You're going to make your way toward a small clearing deep within the mountain, a place where you can pause, reflect, and receive what you need.

How does each part of you respond to this invitation?

What concerns do they have?

What does each one hope to receive?

Take a moment to honor whatever comes up. Without judgment. Without shame. Simply notice.

If any part of you does not wish to go, find out what that part of your soul needs to feel safe. You can stay there with that part of you, knowing God is with you even there.

If these different parts of you are willing, begin walking slowly along a gentle trail.

Notice the pace that feels steady, not rushed.

If you notice any tugging—a worried thought, a to-do list, a distraction—imagine turning toward that part of you and saying:

I see you. I'm here with you.

Notice what shifts when you don't rush or force your soul. When you simply stay steady.

After a few moments, you come to a small clearing deep within the mountain.

It feels open here. Quiet. Safe.

Now, in this clearing, imagine God walking toward you. You might imagine Jesus with his arms open, or God's love like sunlight filtering through the trees.

There is no agenda. God isn't asking you to perform, solve, or prove anything. God is simply moving toward you, delighted to be with you.

Notice what changes inside you when God's presence enters the clearing. Calm. Spaciousness. Warmth. Joy. Or maybe just companionship.

Let yourself feel—even for a moment—that safety of being met and loved exactly as you are. You and the different parts of your soul are not here to be corrected. You are here to be held.

Take a few moments in this clearing with God.

How does each part of you respond to God's presence?

What does each part of you need to receive from God in this moment?

Notice whatever comes. It might be an image, a word, a feeling, or even a friendly silence.

When you're ready, imagine gathering each part of you around you again.

Thank God for drawing near, and for staying near as you go.

Begin your return down the trail, carrying that nearness with you.

As you continue, turn toward each of these parts of you.

Notice how each one has shifted.

Perhaps you notice steadiness.

Perhaps you notice warmth.

Perhaps you simply notice the felt sense of being seen.

Thank each one for walking with you.

Take one more slow breath.

Rest for a moment in gratitude for these parts of you, for yourself, and for God's steady presence.

REFLECTION QUESTIONS

1. As you stood within the hills of your soul mountain, which part or parts of you felt most present?

2. When you invited these parts of your soul to walk with you, what shifted? Did anyone resist or soften?

3. What was it like to lead these parts of you along the trail?

4. Did you sense God's presence in the clearing? If so, what was it like? If not, what did you notice? How did different parts of you respond to God's presence?

5. What shifted as you moved back down the trail?

6. What word, image, or felt sense from this experience do you want to carry with you into your day?

SECURE YOUR SENSE OF WORTH

A secure sense of worth isn't something you muster from within. It is something *bestowed*, something you receive from the One who knit you together with care.

Yet for many of us, worth is where the deepest fractures within our souls live. You might know intellectually that you are loved, but your soul carries older messages that belonging had to be earned, that being chosen was rare, or that your voice was an inconvenience.

When worth feels conditional, different parts of you step in to protect you. Your Controller hustles, trying to secure worth through performance, perfection, or being indispensable. Your Shadow braces for rejection, assuming she'll be overlooked or unwanted. She distracts, criticizes, or endlessly compares you to others around you.

And the Young One is weighed down by your earliest ache to be seen, known, and cherished.

These parts of your soul aren't evidence that something is wrong with you. They are evidence of *longing*, of your soul's deep desire to feel seen, safe, and chosen. When you meet each one with compassion and tend the wounds they carry, something inside you softens. Shame loosens its grip.

You begin to sense a truth rising from the depths of your innermost being:

Your worth was never something to earn.

Your worth was given before you ever lifted a finger.

You have always been—and will always be—God's beloved.

Over time, your inner world begins to orient itself around this truth. You feel less shaken by comparison, less undone by other people's disappointment, and less defined by the betrayals you've endured.

You begin to live from the inner knowing that *you were worth loving all along.*

WHEN YOU FEEL LEFT OUT

Dear one,

I know how sharply it stings when you feel left out. When others gather without you. When invitations don't come. When someone else gets chosen, celebrated, or seen, and it feels as if you're standing just outside the circle.

The pain of rejection is real. It isn't weakness, and it isn't you being "too sensitive." Research suggests that rejection can light up the same part of your brain as physical pain.[1] That's why being left out feels like a punch in the gut. It hurts, because it really does hurt.

I'm sorry you feel left out. It's such a painful ache.

But know that I am here with you.

I know that part of you is tempted to try harder, to bend yourself into knots to fit in. I've seen how hard you've pushed yourself in the past, striving for approval or beating yourself up when it doesn't come.

And I know that when the hurt rises, you've been tempted to shut down, withdraw, or drown your sorrows with quick-fix comforts—things that soothe for a moment but can't give you what you really need.

These reactions make sense. I see how these parts of you are trying to help.

Be gentle with yourself. You don't have to hustle for your worth. You don't have to shrink (or shine) to be loved.

Being left out can make your world feel suddenly small, as if one circle defines your whole story. But this moment is not a measure of your lovability. It's simply one snapshot in a much bigger unfolding. Love is still building a place for you, and it will not require you to disappear to belong.

Let this ache be a signal, not a verdict. Take one slow breath and ask: What would I say to a loved one who felt this way? Then choose one small act of belonging. You might text the friend who feels safe, step outside into the fresh air, or simply place a hand over your heart and let Love meet you there.

Dear one, you were never an afterthought.
You are worthy of being welcomed—again and again and again.
You are beloved.
I am with you now, in this ache, and always.
Nothing about this moment diminishes your worth.
What happened here does not define you.
You belong, and you are held, even here.
With you always,

♡

A PAUSE FOR THE SOUL

If you're feeling left out, take a deep breath and notice what's stirring inside you.
A recent moment when I felt left out was:

A part of me felt:

When I picture this part of me, I see:

The fears/doubts/longings rising in me are:

Another time I felt this way was (recent or long ago):

What was happening then was:

The message I learned or assumed was:

Imagine a younger version of yourself sitting beside you, eyes lowered, unsure if she matters, waiting for someone to see her.

What this part of my soul needs from me is:

What this part of my soul longs to hear from God is:

Let this moment become an act of connection. Instead of reaching outward for reassurance, or turning inward with criticism, stay with the part of you that feels excluded, and offer her the kindness she's always needed.

WHEN YOU'VE BEEN BETRAYED

Dear one,

The pain of betrayal cuts deep. It strikes at the heart of your sense of worth, whispering the lie that you were disposable, unimportant, or easy to replace. It reaches tender places within and leaves you second-guessing yourself and doubting your sense of reality.

When betrayal strikes, different parts of you scramble to make sense of the hurt. Your Controller might replay every moment, searching for what you "should have known," what signals you "should have noticed," or how you "could have prevented" what happened.

Your Shadow tends to absorb the shame, assuming the betrayal must say something about your value or your lovability.

And the Young One inside feels alone and cut off from connection.

Betrayal taps on old wounds: *Why wasn't I worth more? Why am I not enough?*

All the while, I see how you're trying to hold it together, showing up for your people, your friends, and your work. I see the weight you're still holding, even as your soul feels torn and tender.

I hope you can hear me say clearly:

Betrayal says everything about the wound of the betrayer—and nothing about your worth.

You are held by a Love that betrayal cannot undo.

Dear one, let these truths settle deep within your soul:

You did not deserve betrayal.

You were never too little or too much.

You deserved faithfulness, tenderness, and truth.

Your worth remains intact. No one can take it from you.

The wound of betrayal runs deep, but Love runs deeper still.

You do not have to make sense of what happened today.

Or tomorrow.

Or this month.

You do not have to rush to closure, forgiveness, or reconciliation. For now, let it be enough to tell the truth about what happened—and let Love stay with you as you heal.

Little by little, you will gather the wounded parts of your soul and, with God's help, knit them back together in goodness, beauty, and truth.

With you always,

♡

A PAUSE FOR THE SOUL

If you've been betrayed, take a deep breath and notice the stirrings within your soul.

The betrayal I experienced was:

A part of me feels:

When I picture this part of me, I see:

The fears/doubts/longings rising in me are:

Another time I felt this way was (recent or long ago):

What was happening then was:

The lie I started to believe about myself was:

The truth is:

What my soul needs from me as it heals is:

What my soul longs to hear from God is:

Be gentle with yourself. You don't have to force healing or pretend it doesn't hurt. Stay with what's true, and let God meet you right there.

WHEN YOU'RE MISUNDERSTOOD

Dear one,

I know how painful it is when you long to be understood, especially when you're hoping for connection. You explain, and you explain again. And yet you still feel unseen, unheard, or completely misunderstood.

Being misunderstood is a particularly frustrating kind of ache. Sometimes the other person doesn't have the capacity or skills to understand. Sometimes their own fears or defenses get in the way. And sometimes, truly hearing you would require something of them they aren't ready to face.

Whatever the reason, the experience can leave you feeling unsettled and unsure of yourself. Understandably, your Controller works harder, searching for the right words, the perfect explanation, one more angle that might finally make things click. Your Shadow minimizes your feelings, tells you not to care so much, or lashes out in frustration. And the Young One inside remembers other moments when you weren't heard or believed, carrying those memories forward as if they're happening again now.

It's exhausting. And it can also erode something important inside you.

Here's what I want you to know:

Your worth is not secured by being perfectly understood.

When being understood becomes the measure of your worth, you can begin to abandon yourself. You start to overexplain, defend, or reshape what's true just to feel seen. Over time, this pulls you away from your own center.

The most important thing you can do in moments when you feel misunderstood is not to convince someone else but to stay connected to what you know is true inside of you.

Your clarity—your lived experience, your unique perspective, your God-shaped conscience—*doesn't depend on another person's understanding.*

Of course it matters that what you share connects with other people. But what matters most is that you remain faithful to what is honest, loving, and true.

Dear one, your worth doesn't come from being agreed with, affirmed, or perceived accurately at all times. Your worth is already here.

It hurts when others misunderstand you. That grief deserves care. But misunderstanding is not a verdict on your character, your goodness, or your value. This is where integrity lives. It's the strength to stay rooted in truth without hardening your heart or losing yourself.

It's the courage to be honest, the humility to stay open, and the wisdom to know when you've said enough.

As you learn to stay true to yourself while remaining respectful of others, something inside you steadies. You begin to live from a deeper sense of worth, one that doesn't rise and fall with other people's perceptions.

With you always,

♡

A PAUSE FOR THE SOUL

Take a moment to notice what stirs inside when you feel misunderstood.

A recent time I felt misunderstood was:

A part of me feels:

When I picture this part of me, I see:

The fears/doubts/longings rising in me are:

Another time I felt this way was (recent or long ago):

What was happening then was:

The message I learned or assumed was:

What this part of my soul most wants me to understand is:

What this part of my soul most wants God to understand is:

As you pause and tend to this misunderstood part of you, you gain perspective, wisdom, and strength. *You* know what's true, and so does God. From that grounded place, you can rest more securely in your own clarity.

GOING DEEPER: REWRITE THE OLD STORY

This practice is drawn from chapter 9 of *The Secure Soul* and helps you gently rewire the old internal messages attached to unworthiness.

1. Draw a simple timeline across the page. Note two or three key moments when you felt "not chosen" (in childhood, adolescence, or adulthood). You can work with just one if that feels like enough today.

2. Choose one moment from your timeline and reflect on what happened with the perspective and wisdom you didn't have then. What did you do with the pain? How did your Controller or Shadow show up to help you survive?

3. Imagine this younger version of yourself—her age, her posture, the look on her face. If it helps, find a photo of yourself from around that time and simply sit with her. What messages did she pick up about herself back then?

4. What does she most need to hear or receive from you now?

5. Imagine God's presence with this younger part of your soul. How does she respond? What does she want you or God to know, and what does she need to receive? Simply notice whatever arises. Don't force anything that doesn't feel genuine.

6. Take a moment to thank this younger part of you for her presence in your soul. What has she carried for you, and what are you grateful for?

7. Write one simple truth you can return to whenever shame rises. Here are a few examples: *My worth is not earned. I was worth loving all along. I am God's beloved.*

Each time you meet this younger part of you with honesty and tenderness, you loosen the grip of the old story. You are teaching your soul a new way to belong. Little by little, shame loses its grip and Love becomes your home again.

SECURE YOUR SOUL THROUGH INNER REPAIR

Often, we know the ache of feeling let down by others. But the truth is, we also know the ache of disappointing *ourselves.*

It's the sting of regret.

The heaviness of *I wish I had known better.*

The grief of wishing you could redo (or undo) the past.

But a secure soul isn't one that never makes a mistake. A secure soul is one that *knows how to repair*—not only with others, but also within your own soul.

Repair isn't shame or self-flagellation.

Repair isn't minimizing what happened.

Repair isn't blaming your younger self for what she didn't know.

Repair is the sacred art of turning toward what hurts with compassion and with honest naming. It's the courage to face the parts of you that acted out of fear, loneliness, or self-protection. It's the courage to say:

I see you.

I understand why you did that.

I'm here with you now.

It's the humility to invite Love into the wound—to soften it, tend to it, and ultimately heal it.

The process of inner repair is a journey with three movements:

1. Naming what happened without collapsing into shame
2. Meeting the part of you who did her best with what she knew then
3. Honoring what was lost and taking steps to live differently now

This is how a soul becomes secure—not by perfection but by returning to Love, again and again, right where the tear occurred.

WHEN YOU FEEL LIKE YOU'VE FALLEN SHORT

Dear one,

I know how painful it is when you come up against your own limits—when you look back and think, *I thought I'd be further along by now.* When all your effort didn't yield what you'd hoped, or when the gap between who you are and who you want to be feels painfully wide.

Falling short can subtly drain you. It doesn't always surface with one dramatic mistake. Sometimes it comes as a slow form of discouragement. A sense that no matter how much you try, it's never quite enough. You compare yourself to others. You replay what you "should" have done differently. You wonder if something is wrong with you because you're still struggling here.

When this happens, it makes sense that different parts of you step in to manage the ache.

Your Controller might urge you to push harder, to fix yourself, or to set stricter standards. Your Shadow might slip into resignation: *Why bother? You'll just disappoint yourself again.* And the Young One within feels weary and small: *Will I ever be good enough?*

So let me say this:

Falling short doesn't mean you are failing at becoming who you are meant to be.

Growth is rarely linear. Wisdom almost never arrives all at once in a simple bow-tied package. And the measure of a secure soul isn't in how quickly you improve. It's in how you treat yourself when you don't.

You are allowed to be unfinished.

The people we most admire aren't the ones who never fall short. The people we most admire are the ones who fall, learn, grow, and rise again—*returning to Love* every step of the way.

This is the kind of person, the kind of soul, you are becoming.

You are allowed to need time.

You are allowed to learn as you move.

You are allowed to take a pause without giving up.

Inner repair begins right here—with permission to be right where you are. Permission to stop criticizing yourself. Permission to let disappointment in but not to stay forever. Permission to stay connected to Love even when progress feels slow.

Love doesn't rush you past this place. Love meets you in it.

And as you stay here in this discomfort—without collapsing and without striving—something steady grows inside you. You remember that becoming whole isn't about closing every gap. It's about staying rooted in grace while you grow.

Dear one, falling short is not the end of your becoming.

It's part of the long, patient work of learning how to live with honesty, humility, and—always—hope.

With you always,

♡

A PAUSE FOR THE SOUL

If you feel like you've fallen short, take a deep breath and notice the stirrings within your soul.

A part of me feels like I've fallen short when:

____

____

When I picture this part of me, I see:

____

____

The fears/doubts/longings rising in me are:

Another time I felt this way was (recent or long ago):

What was happening then was:

The message I learned or assumed was:

Now imagine yourself with this younger version of you. Or you might imagine what your wisest, gentlest self would say to a beloved child or dear friend who felt this way.

What this part of my soul longs to hear from me is:

What this part of my soul longs to hear from God is:

Slow down and choose kindness toward yourself. Just stay with the tender place, because growth happens in the presence of compassion, not criticism.

WHEN YOU'RE MAD AT YOURSELF

Dear one,

I know how painful that inner blaze can feel, when you're angry with yourself, critical of your choices, or hurt by something you did or didn't do. This kind of inner fury creates a rupture inside your soul, and it needs gentle acknowledgment and tender care.

Anger can feel overwhelming. It's chaotic, consuming, and often louder than any other voice. Inside, different parts of your soul are clashing.

Your Controller might be scolding you: *How could you? You should have known better.* Your Shadow threatens to shut down: *I'm done. I don't even care anymore.* And the Young One absorbs the tension as if you were still a child: *What's wrong with me? I'll never get it right.*

Your anger isn't necessarily wrong, but it can be misguided. You're usually hardest on yourself when you're *already tender*, already vulnerable.

It can feel easier to stay mad at yourself, as if you are the one thing you have control over.

Maybe a part of you believes you deserve it, or that anger is the only way you'll finally listen.

But beneath that initial surge of anger is a pain you're not quite sure how to name—a hurt you'd rather not face. Anger feels energizing in the moment, but it tends to leave sadness on its way out.

The truth is that your anger is a *bid for connection*, signaling that your soul needs your presence, containment, and care.

Sometimes you're mad at yourself because you made a mistake, and what you need is to name what's true and work through a process of repair.

Sometimes your anger shows up as a way of dealing with *someone else's harmful actions*, because blaming yourself feels safer than blaming the person who hurt you.

And sometimes the anger is covering grief—grief for what was lost, what was missed, or what was never within your control to begin with.

So, dear one, don't rush to shut the anger down. And don't hand it the microphone, either. It's here for a reason.

Let it be a signal, not a dictator. Let it point you toward the tender place underneath, the place that needs honesty and care.

You can slow down. You can make room for what's true. You can choose one small act of restoring connection: naming what's hard, offering compassion, or letting God meet you in the very place you feel most disappointed in yourself.

Anger isn't here to destroy you. It's here to reveal what needs healing.

You are capable of repair.

You are worthy of compassion—even from yourself.

And God is big enough to hold you even here.

With you always,

♡

A PAUSE FOR THE SOUL

If you're mad at yourself, take a deep breath and notice the stirrings within.

A part of me is angry because:

____

____

When I picture this part of me, I notice:

____

____

This part of me is trying to help by:

What this part of is afraid might happen is:

Now breathe. Honor the angry part of you, without arguing with her or handing her control.

Now listen for what God says in this moment, remembering that God's voice isn't condemning, nor does it bypass pain. It reflects an honest seeing.

What this part of my soul needs from me or from God is:

The invitation to my soul right now is:

Notice whatever shows up with compassion and care. You don't need to interpret it, override it, or talk yourself out of it. Stay close to the part of you that feels mad and let her tell you what she fears, as well as what she needs.

WHEN YOU'VE DONE SOMETHING WRONG

Dear one,

I know how heavy this feels. Part of you is beating yourself up, and another part wants to hide, hoping it will all just go away. That tug-of-war inside is exhausting.

But it's also a bid for connection.

Please hear me say: Naming what's true—honestly and simply—will *always* set you free.

Hiding from the truth leaves your soul fragmented. Your Controller works overtime trying to make up for the harm caused, without ever addressing the root. Your Shadow works to find ways to minimize or cover it up. When your mistakes stay hidden, disconnection grows within you, with God, and with other people.

You were never meant to carry guilt or shame alone.

Research confirms this. When you hold on to a secret, stress levels increase. But when you share it with someone safe, anxiety lowers, intimacy increases, and your overall sense of well-being improves.[1] Scripture calls this confession. Neuroscientists describe it as a way of relieving the brain, freeing up energy that was tied up in hiding.

That's why confession often includes telling another person. Be wise about it. Don't entrust your tender pearl of confession to just anyone. Not everyone is safe enough to hold it.

But naming the truth out loud—with someone safe—breaks shame's grip and makes space for trust and healing. It doesn't have to be complicated or dramatic. You don't have to overexplain. Just say something simple: "I've made a mistake. I wanted to be honest with you." Sharing truth with another trustworthy person strengthens bonds and *increases intimacy.*

Dear one, when you bring what's true into the light, connection with yourself and with God deepens, even if human connection takes time to repair. When you whisper honestly, "This is where I've fallen short. This is where I need help," you open a door.

Instead of rejection, you meet presence.

Instead of condemnation, you meet compassion.

Connection grows.

Confession isn't groveling.

It isn't self-flagellation.

It's recognizing *your part* in disconnection.

It's learning to return to Love, even then, especially then.

And here is the miracle: Every time you bring your whole self into the light, Love rushes in to heal.

With you always,

♡

A PAUSE FOR THE SOUL

When you've done something wrong, take a deep breath and notice the stirrings within.

What happened was (just state the facts, simple and clear):

The part of me that acted out was trying to (protect me, keep me safe, avoid pain, etc.):

The feelings coming up are:

When I was young, what happened when I did something wrong was:

The old message I'm tempted to believe is:

Now picture whispering your mistake honestly to God—without excuses and without fear, remembering that it's God's kindness that leads to repentance (Rom. 2:4).

When I imagine bringing a mistake or shortcoming to God, I fear God might say:

I hope God might say:

What I want to say to God is:

A safe person I could trust with the truth of what happened is:

Let yourself be honest and gentle here. No scrambling to fix, no rushing to move on. Stay with the part of you that feels regret and let her tell you what she's carrying.

GOING DEEPER: REPAIR AN INNER RUPTURE

This exercise helps you tend to ruptures inside your inner world using the three movements of repair from chapter 10 of *The Secure Soul.* You can work through these steps when you're mad at yourself, when you've done something wrong, when regret lingers, when a memory keeps replaying, or when something feels unsettled inside.

Take a breath. Let one moment come to mind, from the past or from the present. Then move through the steps below, slowly and honestly.

1. Name what happened.

What are the facts—just what happened, without analysis or interpretation?

What do you notice in your body? What feelings arise within you?

2. Meet the part of you who did her best with what she knew.

Which part of you showed up? How old is she and how was she trying to help?

How do you feel toward her? When you turn toward her with kindness, how does she respond?

If it feels helpful, connect with God in this moment. How does she respond to God's presence?

3. Honor what was lost and choose a different way forward.

What did she need in that moment that she didn't receive?

What do you want her to know about who you are becoming?

How might you show up differently now?

The goal of this exercise is to build trust within your soul between a part of you who was still in process and your wiser self—the person you are becoming.

This is integration. It's what creates a secure soul not through erasing the past, but through reclaiming every part of you with gentleness and truth in partnership with God's Spirit.

SECURE YOUR SOUL THROUGH RISK

There are seasons in every soul's life when something inside begins to shift. A restlessness.

A longing. An ache that whispers, *Something needs to change.*

But so often, even when the desire for change is real, taking a risk can feel terrifying. Not because you're weak, but because your inner world *remembers* what instability once felt like.

Somewhere along the way, you learned to survive by staying small, staying comfortable, staying close to what was familiar, even when the familiar was unhealthy, constricting, or no longer life-giving.

But now, when a new opportunity or possibility appears, your soul remembers those old rules:

Don't rock the boat.

Don't hope for too much.

Don't leave what you know.

Don't make a mistake you can't undo.

A secure soul doesn't pretend that risks aren't vulnerable. It doesn't take risks recklessly.

A secure soul *leads with wisdom, openness, and a deep trust that growth is possible.*

Here's the thing: Healthy risk rarely starts with a dramatic leap. It starts by building *inner safety*, tending to the fears within, and anchoring your inner world in God's steady presence.

The secure soul knows that risk is a sacred unfolding of courage:

- The courage to tell the truth
- The courage to set a boundary
- The courage to stay when staying is harder than leaving
- The courage to leave when leaving is harder than staying
- The courage to grow beyond who you used to be

Ultimately, a secure soul risks because *she knows she is held by Love, no matter the outcome.*

WHEN YOU'RE AFRAID TO MAKE A CHANGE

Dear one,

I know how unsettling it feels when change is on the horizon. You feel the pull toward something new, but also the pull toward what you might leave behind. You want courage and you also want certainty. The problem is that those two things don't typically arrive together.

Maybe the change is something external. It might be a new job, a move, a relationship shifting, a child leaving home, or a season of caregiving beginning (or ending).

Or maybe it's something you notice inside you, a growing desire you can't ignore, a longing for rest, a need for more space, a sense that you've outgrown a role you've carried for years, or the realization that staying the same is becoming more painful than risking something new.

These changes are tender places. And even when the change is the next right move to make, not everything inside you will feel ready at the same time.

Your Controller worries, analyzes, perfects, or plans, trying to account for every possible outcome. She tries to talk you into (or out of) the change. Your Shadow distracts you or tries to minimize the impact. She sometimes compares your path to others' in a shaming way. Meanwhile, the Young One remembers the uncertainty of change from the past. She doesn't just fear change—she fears being alone inside it.

Change itself doesn't have to be a threat. It can become an invitation.

Dear one, navigating change bravely doesn't require certainty. But it does require *connection.* Not connection to the perfect plan. Connection to what's true inside you—and to the God who stays.

Remember: You don't have to leap. You only have to take the next brave step. And "brave" doesn't mean big. It means honest.

You don't have to move impulsively or recklessly.

You don't have to numb yourself to escape discomfort.

You don't have to let worry or anxiety take the lead.

Instead, begin with one simple question:

What is the next step I can take without abandoning a part of myself?

Then listen for your inner pacing—not the urgency of fear, but the steadiness of wisdom. Fear feels tightening and frantic. Wisdom feels steady, even when it's slow or costly.

If your Controller is anxious, offer her a job that truly helps: *Help me take one step—not solve the whole future.*

If your Shadow is pulling you to numb, gently return to the present: *What am I trying not to feel right now?*

If the Young One is scared, offer her safety: a hand on your heart, a slow breath, a whispered reminder: *I'm here. You're not alone.*

And if you're unsure what the "next brave step" is, make it small:

- Gather one piece of information.
- Have one honest conversation.
- Set one boundary that creates breathing room.
- Take one day to pray and notice what brings steadiness rather than spiraling.

You're not looking for certainty. You're looking for enough steadiness to take one true step. And you can trust this: God meets you there in that next step, not only at the final outcome.

With you always,

♡

A PAUSE FOR THE SOUL

If you're afraid to make a change, take a deep breath and notice the stirrings within. The change I'm sensing I might need to make is:

A part of me fears:

Another part of me longs for:

Another time I felt this way was (recent or long ago):

What happened then was:

The message I learned or assumed was:

What I found helpful was:

What the fearful part of my soul needs from me or from God is:

What the longing part of my soul needs from me or from God is:

Let yourself pause here at the edge of change. No forcing, no shaming, no rushing. Simply be with the part of you that hesitates and listen for what she needs to feel safe.

WHEN YOU CAN'T LET GO

Dear one,

I know how urgent it feels when you so desperately want to fix something—or someone. A part of you scrambles to keep everything running smoothly, to keep everyone feeling okay. Somewhere along the way, you learned that love and safety come through *managing other people's reactions, emotions, and problems.*

So often, a part of you slips into overfunctioning. To you, it feels normal—almost automatic. You read the room. You know what feelings lie beneath a few words, a pause, or a tone. You sense what's coming before anyone says it out loud.

Almost effortlessly, you are working so hard to:

- Fix problems that were never yours to fix
- Push yourself to earn approval
- Manage conversations so conflict doesn't surface
- Step in quickly so no one else has to feel discomfort
- Always show up as the strong one

But here's the truth: When this hardworking Controller part of you overfunctions, she often stirs awake your Shadow. I see that part of you working so hard to keep it together. But I also see another place within you rising up in resentment—pulling back, numbing, or checking out when it all feels like too much. Not exactly a great setup, is it?

I get that you're trying to help. But right now all of your hard efforts are out of balance. Jesus said to love others as yourself. And somewhere along the way, you left *yourself* out of the equation.

Letting go isn't losing control. Instead, it's learning to trust that you don't have to carry everything alone. It's learning what's actually yours to steward with love, and learning how to release the rest.

Dear one, letting go doesn't mean you stop caring. It doesn't mean you've given up. It means you are learning to care *wisely*.

Love does not ask you to carry what was never yours to bear. Some things are burdens meant to be shared: moments of grief, pain, or overwhelm where your presence matters more than your ability to fix. Other things are meant for each person to carry themselves: choices, growth, and emotional work.

Wisdom lives in knowing the difference. When you honor that line, love becomes clearer, lighter, and more sustainable. You can stay connected without disappearing, generous without overreaching, present without abandoning yourself. And that kind of love leaves room for rest.

You learn that true safety doesn't come from managing, performing, or working overtime to keep the peace. It comes from presence—from the steady, unshakable Love that meets you in your time of need and frees you to offer what is truly yours to give.

With you always,

A PAUSE FOR THE SOUL

If you can't let go, take a deep breath and notice the stirrings within.
What I can't let go of is:

One thing I do when I'm hanging on to control is:

This part of me fears:

The deeper longing beneath is:

What I respect about this part of me hanging on is:

What I wish she could release is:

Another time I felt this way was (recent or long ago):

The message I learned or assumed was:

Now imagine speaking to this hardworking part of you as kindly as you would to a friend. What this part of my soul needs to hear from me is:

What this part of my soul longs to hear from God is:

Notice whatever shows up with compassion and curiosity. You don't need to let go all at once; you let go one deep breath at a time.

WHEN YOU FEEL CONFLICTED

Dear one,

Oh, how I hate to see you so conflicted! But I understand. Sometimes the hardest battles we face are not with other people but within ourselves.

I see how one part of you pulls you in one direction, wanting you to take a certain path, insisting it's the right or responsible thing to do. All the while, another part of you is tugging just as strongly in the opposite direction, raising doubts, surfacing fears, remembering past pain, or pointing out costs.

And you feel stuck. Not because you're weak or indecisive, but because you're standing at an inner crossroads.

Here's what I want you to know: Conflict inside you doesn't mean you're doing something wrong. It's a sign that more than one truth is present. And wisdom doesn't come from silencing one voice so another can win. It comes from slowing down long enough to listen.

Each part of you that's showing up right now is there for a reason. One may be trying to protect you from regret, while another may be guarding your values. One may be holding grief, while another feels ready to move forward.

These parts of you are carriers of information.

When you rush yourself toward a decision, you don't actually get peace—you get relief that doesn't last. But when you pause and begin to name what each part is afraid of losing or hoping to protect, something gentler happens. Your nervous system settles. Creativity kicks in. Clarity starts to break through.

This is holy ground. It's a place that doesn't necessarily offer quick answers but one that asks for honest attention.

Instead of asking, *What's the right answer?* ask, *What is each part of me trying to tell me?*

Clarity often comes after connection, including connection within yourself.

The presence of conflicted feelings doesn't mean you don't care; that's indifference.

Being conflicted usually means you can see real truths on more than one side. And that complexity is a strength. People who carry more inner conflict are often less impulsive, more perceptive, more creative, and more fair-minded—beautiful qualities you don't want to lose.[1]

You don't have to resolve everything today.

You don't have to force alignment before it's ready.

Your task right now is simpler and braver: to listen without judgment, to name the different perspectives, and to trust that wisdom unfolds when all voices are allowed to speak.

I'm here with you at the crossroads.

With you always,

♡

A PAUSE FOR THE SOUL

If your soul feels conflicted, take a deep breath and notice the stirrings within.

What I'm conflicted about is:

One part of me says:

Another part of me says:

When you're conflicted, there's often a deeper fear or tender vulnerability underneath. The deeper fear underneath is:

Now imagine gathering both of these parts, as if you were hosting them at the same table. Let them speak without judgment. Let them feel seen.

What each part is longing for is:

What they most need from my wiser adult self or from God is:

Notice what emerges with compassion and patience. When each part of you is welcomed and heard, wisdom begins to take shape.

GOING DEEPER: GATHER YOUR SOUL AT THE TABLE

In chapter 11 of *The Secure Soul*, I describe a moment of inner turmoil just before I took a risk. I could feel different parts of me stirring. One part of me wanted to perfect, another kept criticizing me, and a tender part felt exposed. This exercise helps you navigate moments like that by gathering the different parts of your soul in connection rather than letting one take over.

Take a breath. Think of a current situation that leaves you feeling stuck, conflicted, or uncertain about a decision.

Which parts of you seem most active? You might name them in your own words (the Worrier, the Pleaser, the Fighter). Or you may recognize the Controller, the Shadow, or the Young One.

- Part A: ____________________________
- Part B: ____________________________

Now imagine each of these parts seated around a table within your soul. There is space for each one. No one is rushed. No one is shamed.

Gently turn toward Part A. How does she show up in this moment—her tone, her posture, her energy? What is she urging you to do, what does she fear, and what does she most long for?

When Part A feels heard, imagine her settling back into her chair, fully seen and valued.

Now turn your attention to Part B. How does she show up in this moment—her tone, her posture, her energy? What is she urging you to do, what does she fear, and what does she most long for?

You're not solving the tension yet. You are simply allowing each voice to be heard in safety.

Linger long enough to sense the genuine concerns beneath each part's urgency. Often, what looks like conflict on the surface is a shared longing underneath.

Now imagine God's loving presence steady at the table—not to take sides, but to hold the whole of you.

What does each part need to receive—from you or from God?

What word, metaphor, or image do you want to carry with you—something that anchors you in a sense of wholeness?

Let that word or image settle into your body as a reminder that you can move forward with your whole soul held in Love.

If one small next step becomes clear, write it here:

Before you leave the table, pause for a moment. What do you notice? What shifed within?

When your whole soul feels heard and seen, wisdom—and the courage to act—grows naturally in that space of connection.

SECURE YOUR SOUL THROUGH TRANSITION

There are times in life when you sense a shift inside you long before you can name it. It might be a restlessness, a loosening, or an inner knowing: *Something is changing, and I'm not sure where I fit yet.*

Change is what happens around you: an event, a shift, a new circumstance. Transition, on the other hand, is what happens within you as you respond to that change. It arrives with a tender kind of disorientation.[1]

You often feel the fragility of transition before you can make sense of it. The familiarity of the past (or present) doesn't feel as comforting as it once did, but the new chapter of your life hasn't yet taken shape.

Parts of you long for clarity, grounding, and steadiness, but instead your soul feels awkward or wobbly—like you can't quite find your bearings. You're somewhere between an ending and a new beginning.

These in-between spaces are unsettling. You might feel unsteady, unsure, or a bit untethered. You might even wonder if something is wrong with you for not feeling stable, prepared, or "on top of your game."

But feeling "in-between" doesn't mean you're lost. It means you're in transition. And transition invites you into a different kind of security, a different kind of trust. It's a season that calls for extra kindness toward your soul, precisely because the usual cues of safety are harder to find.

A secure soul doesn't rush to prevent or escape the discomfort of transition.

It pauses.

It slows.

It listens for what's tender within.

And it allows God to carefully re-root the soul in new soil, one faithful step at a time.

WHEN YOU FEEL FAR FROM HOME

Dear one,

I know how disorienting it feels when "home" is somewhere you can no longer touch with your hands, see with your eyes, or smell the familiar scents. Maybe it's a childhood house, a beloved city, a neighborhood that shaped you, or a landscape that once held your soul steady.

When you're far from that place, something deep inside feels tender. It's more than homesickness. It's your nervous system noticing the loss of what was familiar—what once told your body, without words, *You're safe here.*

The places that raised us anchored our souls too. Places shape us. They hold our memories, our becoming, our first tastes of love or loss. They serve as a witness to the movements of our lives, especially when we were young.

So *of course* you feel the ache when you are far from the place that once felt like home. That ache doesn't mean you're stuck. It means you've experienced a secure attachment—yes, even with a place.

Different parts of your soul try to navigate that ache differently. Your Controller tries to re-create the familiar, trying to keep life predictable enough so the ground feels steady again. Your Shadow minimizes the ache or searches for something new to fill the void. Meanwhile, the Young One inside simply *misses what felt familiar and safe*, longing for the smells, the sounds, the rhythms that once made her feel rooted. If you notice these parts of you stirring, be gentle with yourself. They're trying to help you find your footing.

Feeling far from home can awaken grief, but it can also awaken gratitude. Often, the two are tangled up together.

Here's what I want you to remember: Home is not only a place on a map. Home is a kind of "secure base"—an attachment tether. It's the physical representation of being held in steady love, known, and connected. And while you can't always return to a particular address, you can learn to create pockets of safety that help your body and soul settle.

Start with small acts of planting new roots. Find one familiar anchor you can return to. It might be a walk at the same time each day, a corner of your space that feels like "yours," a text to someone who feels safe, or a prayer you don't have to work hard to say. This anchor doesn't replace what you lost, but it does give your soul somewhere to land.

Over time, you learn to carry a sense of home within you.

A rootedness.

A belonging that doesn't vanish when the landscape shifts.

A steadiness that travels with you.

Even here, God is not far. And you are not as untethered as you feel.

With you always,

A PAUSE FOR THE SOUL

If you feel far from home, take a deep breath and notice the stirrings within.

The home that feels far away right now is (a place, a person, a season, a community, etc.):

A part of me feels:

When I picture this part of me, I see:

The fears/griefs/longings rising in me are:

Another time I felt this way was (recent or long ago):

The message I learned or assumed was:

What I need to feel held where I am is:

Now imagine God drawing near—not to rush you, fix you, or tell you to move on, but to sit beside the place in you that feels displaced.

What this part of my soul longs to hear from God is:

Stay with whatever shows up. You don't need to fix or analyze—simply keep this part of your soul company as she shares her experience with you.

WHEN YOU FEEL UNTETHERED

Dear one,

I remember a season in my twenties, after leaving college, when I felt untethered from everything I knew. My friends were scattered across different states, and my parents had sold the home of my childhood and moved far away, so there was no real sense of "home" to return to. I didn't yet know what I wanted to do with my life, and I had no idea where to land. I hadn't realized how quietly all the change had stacked up.

Feeling untethered or unmoored inside can sneak up on you. It happens when several anchors disappear at once, and your soul hasn't had time to form new ones. Your people are scattered. Your routines are disrupted. The place that once held your memories is no longer accessible. The next season hasn't yet taken shape. When your anchors go, your nervous system stays on watch, scanning for the next place it can safely rest.

The good news is that when your body is on watch, you can offer it something grounding: small, intentional anchors that remind you you're not alone. In my case, I became so anxious it was hard to sleep. One night, I imagined the faces of loving friends—each one someone who had carried me through a hard time. I surrounded myself with those images and let their love soothe me into rest, even though they were far away.

I didn't know it then, but I was engaging in something research supports: the power of imagination to regulate the nervous system. Simply calling to mind the face of someone safe can activate the same pathways in your brain as if they were with you, offering comfort, grounding, and connection.

Imagination is one way to signal safety from within. You can also learn to notice and receive the small tethers of connection woven into your day, those tiny moments when your shoulders drop or you find yourself taking a breath. Even the smallest signals of connection—a kind look in a stranger's eye, a neighbor's smile, someone saying your name—register deeply. They remind you: Connection isn't far off. Connection is right here.

And remember that you can also become a tether of connection for someone else. Offer a smile. Speak a name. Hold eye contact just a beat longer. These simple acts don't only bring connection to others; they also root and restore something inside you.

Because the truth is, even in the in-between places, God is weaving cords of connectedness everywhere around you.

With you always,

♡

A PAUSE FOR THE SOUL

If you feel untethered, take a deep breath and notice the stirrings within.

A part of my soul feels (lonely, unmoored, anxious, tender, searching, disoriented, etc.):

The message I tell myself sounds like (*I don't know where I belong, I feel far away, I miss something I can't name*, etc.):

My heart longs for (home, familiarity, steadiness, warmth, connection, something real, etc.):

I feel this most in my body in my (chest, stomach, throat, shoulders, whole body, etc.):

Another time I felt this way was (recent or long ago):

Now let your imagination become a bridge. Picture a person or place that has felt steady or safe to you. It might be the face of someone who has loved you well. It might be a room, a landscape, a favorite trail, or even a memory of a moment when you felt calm.

The person or place I'm imagining is:

What I feel when I picture this is:

Let that feeling settle into your body. Let it remind you of God's nearness.

What this part of my soul needs from me right now is:

Stay here for a moment. Let your body take in what feels grounded.

WHEN YOU'RE SURPRISED BY WHO SHOWS UP

Dear one,

I know how confusing it feels when God doesn't send the people you expected to meet you in this season. Sometimes the ones you most hoped would show up—don't. And sometimes the care you need arrives through people you never imagined would carry it.

When I was new to graduate school, I felt overwhelmed by all I was learning in my psychology program. At the same time, I was struggling to connect with a faith community. In that season, I rented an apartment from an eighty-two-year-old woman, someone whose life and background were completely different from my own. And yet she was the one who showed up for me in ways I didn't know I needed.

One Friday evening, I accepted her invitation to dinner, a part of me thinking it would be kind to spend time with this older woman. But I quickly realized it wasn't me offering care—it was her. As I found myself sharing some of my struggles, she listened quietly and then said, almost in passing: "I wonder what God is doing in your life."

It was such a simple statement, but it cut through the noise of my confusion. Through her presence, I caught a glimpse of God's nearness. She reminded me that God often shows his love in surprising ways, not always in the ways we might expect.

Maybe you've experienced something like that too. It might be someone you didn't think you had much in common with, yet they're the one who keeps showing up. It could be a family member you've written off as too different or too much; yet somehow, they offer kindness at exactly the right moment.

In my experience, there are two kinds of people who help us heal and grow when we're feeling disconnected from ourselves, from others, and from God.

Attachment figures are the steady ones. They provide nurture and consistency, wiring your nervous system for safety and connection. Their gift is stability: a secure base you can return to. They might be a parent, a sibling, a spouse, a friend, or a mentor—someone you've come to rely on.

Liminal figures are the surprising ones. They appear at the threshold of change, often outside your closest circle, or outside any circle you imagined might be yours. Because they don't share your history, they can sometimes see your story more clearly. Their gift is invitation: holding a lantern at the edge of your story, illuminating new possibilities.

Both kinds of people are essential. Attachment figures help you feel rooted. Liminal figures help you stretch and grow.

Dear one, don't be surprised if God's care comes wrapped in unexpected people.

Sometimes healing flows through a parent, partner, or trusted friend; other times, it arrives through someone you never expected to need—or to trust.

Each one is a reminder: God provides love in more ways than you can imagine.

With you always,

A PAUSE FOR THE SOUL

If you're surprised by who is (or isn't) showing up, take a deep breath and notice the stirrings within.

A specific time when I needed support was:

The person or community a part of me hoped would show up was:

What I felt when they didn't show up was:

What this part of me longed to feel from them was:

The messages I told myself about their absence were:

The person or community who did show up was:

What I learned from their presence is:

The gift this person or community brought to a part of my soul was:

What I want to carry forward from this is:

Notice what this reveals about what your soul needs, and how God meets you. Stay open to receiving care, and offering it, in surprising places.

GOING DEEPER: ANCHOR YOUR SOUL IN A PLACE

The following exercises help you anchor your soul in a place, drawing on themes from chapter 12 of *The Secure Soul*. Work through the ones that feel most helpful. There's no need to do them all at once.

1. Envision or call to mind a place where a part of your soul felt connected, loved, and at home. Let yourself settle into it: What do you see, hear, smell, or touch? Who is there with you?

Gather images, objects, and photographs that remind you of this place. It could be anything that helps this part of your soul remember the groundedness and comfort it felt.

Now stay with these reminders for thirty seconds longer than you want to. Let your soul take each one in: Notice your breathing, your shoulders, your chest. Notice any emotions that surface.

What do you notice?

Return to these reminders whenever the feeling of being untethered spikes. Over time, this part of your soul learns to return to safety through repeated, small reminders.

2. Pay attention to the small signs of connection in your daily rhythms:

Who are the people whose presence feels grounding or familiar—the ones you see regularly in ordinary places? What places or routines help your body settle?

When someone acknowledges you by name, a smile, or eye contact—or when you notice a familiar sound, place, or memory—what do you notice in your body?

Do you notice any resistance to receiving these small tethers—maybe a voice that dismisses them as too small or not enough? What does it say?

Imagine each small tether as God's way of whispering: *You are not alone. You belong here.*

3. Read Psalm 23 slowly. Then rewrite it from the perspective of a place where a part of your soul has felt connected, loved, and at home. You can use the place you pictured in step 1. Let the imagery of that place mingle with the promises of the Shepherd.

Take a moment to write your version here:

4. Write a thank-you letter (sent or unsent) to someone unexpected who carried light for you at a crucial moment on your journey. Offering gratitude strengthens connection, both with them and within your own soul.

The person I want to thank is:

SECURE YOUR SOUL IN RELATIONSHIPS

When your own soul is secure, you're more able to form healthy relationships with others, ones marked by authenticity, intimacy, and the ability to repair when things go wrong.

A secure soul doesn't require perfect relationships. It's formed inside you first through inner attunement, tending what hurts, staying connected to God, and learning the language of your own internal world. As you practice these skills inwardly, they begin to shape how you show up with others.

You start to recognize when someone is truly reliable, safe, or trustworthy. And you learn to speak up for your soul when someone lets you down.

In short, when you build trust within yourself, you're more equipped to enter into trusting relationships with others.

A secure soul in relationships:

- Stays present without needing to control, convince, or disappear.
- Holds on to itself—reflects its values, its needs, its longings—while still making room for differences in someone else.

- Recognizes the bids for connection beneath conflict, criticism, misunderstandings, and even silence.
- Returns to Love again and again—first within yourself, then with others—inviting God's presence to steady what happens between you.

Relationships will still reveal your inner needs, activate old patterns, and stir your deepest attachment wounds. But they also offer daily invitations to stay grounded, connected, curious, and true.

WHEN YOU'VE DISAPPOINTED SOMEONE

Dear one,

There are few feelings more unsettling than sensing you've disappointed someone. Your stomach drops. Your chest tightens. A part of you scrambles to fix it, while another part wants to hide.

This moment often activates familiar patterns from long ago.

Your Controller rushes in to manage the situation—apologizing too quickly, over-explaining, trying to smooth things over—before you've paused to ask an important question: *Have I actually done something wrong, or have I simply bumped up against my own limits?*

Your Shadow interprets someone's disappointment as proof that you're too much, not enough, or difficult to love, as if their discomfort must mean that you've failed.

And the Young One remembers earlier moments when someone's disappointment felt dangerous, when disapproval led to withdrawal, anger, or loss of connection. Your soul reacts as if those stakes are still present now.

Please hear me say:

Someone else's disappointment does not automatically mean you've done something wrong.

When you disappoint someone, the most important work isn't to rush into fixing. It's to stay connected to *truth*.

We all disappoint other people. And we are all disappointed at times. Disappointment isn't necessarily a sign of relational rupture; it's part of honest, adult relationships. So when you're on the receiving end of someone's frustration, sadness, or disappointment, take a moment to pause and discern:

Did I act outside of my values—or did I honor a boundary?

Did I cause harm—or did I simply stay within my limits?

Is repair needed—or is this discomfort something the other person has to carry?

Sometimes disappointing someone means an apology is needed.

And sometimes disappointing someone means you've done something brave.

Learning to tolerate someone else's disappointment—without collapsing, defending, or retreating—is a sign of a growing, secure soul. It's how you stay present to yourself and present to the other person, without abandoning either one.

So as you notice the discomfort that arises when someone is let down, return to what is steady and true:

You are allowed to have limits.

You are allowed to say no.

You are allowed to choose what is right for you, even when someone else feels unhappy about it.

Your work is not to prevent disappointment at all costs. Your work is to remain grounded, honest, and connected, even when the moment is uncomfortable.

Because even here, you are held.

With you always,

♡

A PAUSE FOR THE SOUL

If you feel like you've disappointed someone, take a deep breath and notice the stirrings within.

The feelings that come up when I've disappointed someone are:

____

____

When I picture this part of me, I see:

____

____

What this part of me fears is:

Another time I felt this way was (recent or long ago):

The message I learned or assumed was:

What's true in this situation is:

What *is* mine to own is:

What's *not* mine to own is:

God's invitation to me is:

Often, the fear underneath is bigger than the situation itself. What helps most isn't pressure but perspective: Love isn't fragile, even when someone else's disappointment feels loud.

WHEN YOU FEEL RESENTFUL

Dear one,

I know that slow burn inside you: the tightness in your chest, the quips on the tip of your tongue, the sense that you're carrying far more than your share.

Resentment creeps in quietly at first, but over time it grows heavy and sharp. It's the feeling that you've been giving and giving, while someone or something keeps taking more than it returns.

Resentment is often misguided, but it's there for a reason. It's a signal that a part of your soul has been *overfunctioning* while another part has gone unheard or unseen. Your Controller steps in to hold everything together, insisting you can handle it. Your Shadow simmers and mutters, *This isn't fair.* And the Young One inside feels overlooked, unprotected, or taken for granted.

And meanwhile—as all this commotion is happening inside you—nothing is actually getting resolved in the relationship. Maybe a stray sarcastic remark slips out. But you quickly apologize for it or swallow it down again.

Resentment doesn't make you unkind. It doesn't make you selfish. It reveals a place where love has gotten lopsided. Where your voice, your needs, or your limits have been ignored, minimized, or silenced—often by *you*.

You're not wrong for feeling resentful, dear one. But I do want you to pay attention to it.

Resentment can erode your soul and your relationships. But it's also a guide, showing you where healing, honesty, or boundaries are needed.

When you notice resentment, slow down. Pay attention. Don't scramble to cover it over. Instead, consider what your soul needs most right now:

- Courage to name what's not working
- Permission to rest
- Wisdom to know what needs to change
- Grace to carry what's yours—and to release what isn't
- Gentleness for the part of you that feels unseen or unappreciated

Resentment doesn't disappear by pushing it down; it transforms when you honor the truth it reveals.

Even in the heat of resentment, you are held by Love.

With you always,

A PAUSE FOR THE SOUL

If you're feeling resentful, take a deep breath and notice what's stirring within.

A recent moment when I noticed resentment was:

A part of me feels:

When I picture this part of me, I see:

The fears/doubts/longings rising in me are:

Another time I felt this way was (recent or long ago):

What was happening then was:

The message I learned or assumed was:

The truth is:

The moments when I feel most honored or seen are:

What this part of my soul needs from me is:

What this part of my soul needs from God is:

One boundary that would bring breathing room is:

Notice whatever shows up with compassion and care. Be gentle as you listen inward, and let one clear boundary take shape, just enough for today.

WHEN YOU WANT TO AVOID CONFLICT

Dear one,

I know how tempting it is to pull away when something feels hard. A part of you whispers, *Just let it go. Stay quiet. Don't make waves.* It feels safer—or at least more comfortable—in the moment to tuck your feelings away, to sidestep the conversation, or to convince yourself it's not worth it.

And sometimes, that's true. Sometimes choosing to let something go really is wisdom. But the key word is *choosing*. To let something go is a decision, a conscious act of love and trust. You recognize, This isn't worth my energy right now. You trust that you'll return to it later if needed. You have safe outlets to process your feelings. You can release it without building resentment.

But other times, it's not really letting go—it's *avoiding*. You stay silent, not out of freedom, but out of fear. You tell yourself it's no big deal, but inside it eats at you. You start to adjust to patterns that actually harm you or the relationship. And you end up harboring unspoken resentment that seeps into other corners of your heart.

I see how heavy that becomes for you. Avoidance feels like self-protection, but it leaves you lonelier over time. It robs you of the very connection you long for.

Dear one, avoiding conflict doesn't make you weak. It reveals where your soul still longs for safety. When you meet that longing with compassion and God's presence, you become more anchored, more grounded, more capable of engaging conflict with courage.

Sometimes engaging conflict begins by writing down one honest sentence you want to say. You can then practice it until it feels possible to speak.

When you notice this pull to avoid, slow down. Pay attention. Don't let it lull you into entropy. Instead, consider what your soul needs most right now, even here in the avoidance:

- Compassion for your fear
- Clarity to know when to speak up—and when to wait
- Wisdom to choose the right moment
- Discernment to ask for support
- Courage to be direct

And remember, you don't step into conflict alone. Love goes with you.
With you always,

♡

A PAUSE FOR THE SOUL

Take a moment to notice what stirs inside when you're wanting to avoid conflict.
A recent moment when I wanted to avoid conflict was:

When I imagine myself addressing it, I feel:

When I picture this part of me, I see:

The story I am telling myself about what will happen is:

Another time I felt this way was (recent or long ago):

What was happening then was:

The message I learned or assumed was:

The moments I feel most empowered to speak are when:

What this part of my soul needs from me is:

What this part of me needs from God is:

Stay here a moment longer. You don't have to push yourself into conflict. Just stay present with what's asking for your attention and let one brave next step form.

GOING DEEPER: SPEAK UP ON BEHALF OF YOUR SOUL

Any time connection feels strained—when you're misunderstood, avoiding conflict, or feeling resentful—different parts of you rise up with fear, longing, or old stories. Drawing on chapter 13 of *The Secure Soul*, this practice helps you listen to those parts of your soul so you can speak up with clarity, courage, and compassion in your relationships.

1. Recall a recent moment when you stayed quiet instead of speaking up.

What was happening?

What did you hold back?

What did a part of you fear might happen?

How was this part of you trying to help?

2. Bring to mind a moment from childhood when you tried to speak up for yourself. What happened?

Imagine this young part of your soul. Maybe she's small, sincere, or trying to be brave. What message did she pick up about using her voice?

What does she need from you?

3. Now, if it's helpful, imagine God entering that scene with you. Not correcting. Not shaming. Simply reinforcing your dignity, your voice, and your belonging.

How does this part of you respond to God's presence?

What quality does she long to receive?

4. Return slowly to your present situation.

What is one small, honest way you can speak up for yourself? *(Writing down what you wish you could say, naming one honest feeling, stating a small limit, saying "That hurt" without explaining it away, etc.)*

What would help your body feel grounded enough to say what you need to say?

Write down a short sentence or phrase that meets your soul's place of need. Imagine it coming from a voice of tenderness and truth. It could be from your wisest self, from the steady presence of Love, or from someone trustworthy. *(You don't have to disappear to keep peace; You can be honest without being harsh; I'm proud of you.)*

Let this sentence become an anchor you can return to before, during, and after hard conversations.

Speaking up on behalf of yourself isn't about winning or convincing. It's about *showing up for your own soul* with God beside you. It's about letting courage and wisdom grow from the steadiness of being held.

NOTES

1. Chuck DeGroat, *Healing What's Within: Coming Home to Yourself—and to God—When You're Weary, Wounded, and Wandering* (Tyndale Refresh, 2024), 7–8.
2. The concept of recurring family roles is rooted in family systems theory and has been further developed in addiction and relational literature. See Murray Bowen, *Family Therapy in Clinical Practice* (Jason Aronson, 1978); and Claudia Black, *It Will Never Happen to Me!: Children of Alcoholics as Youngsters—Adolescents—Adults* (Ballantine Books, 1981).
3. My understanding of "parts" is informed by Dr. Richard Schwartz and the Internal Family Systems (IFS) model, which describes three broad categories of parts—managers, firefighters, and exiles. In this workbook, however, I am developing a simplified and spiritually integrated template of three parts that reflects my own observations and theological commitments. My use of the phrase "bids for connection" is informed by John Gottman's work on relational bids. See Richard C. Schwartz, *Introduction to the Internal Family Systems Model* (Trailheads, 2001); and John M. Gottman and Joan DeClaire, *The Relationship Cure: A 5 Step Guide to Strengthening Your Marriage, Family, and Friendships* (Random House, 2002), 4.
4. For more on loving your inner enemies, see Alison Cook and Kimberly Miller, *Boundaries for Your Soul: How to Turn Your Overwhelming Thoughts and Feelings into Your Greatest Allies* (Nelson Books, 2018), 58–59.
5. Julia Cameron, *The Artist's Way: A Spiritual Path to Higher Creativity*, 30th anniversary ed. (Tarcher, 2016), 18.
6. St. John of the Cross, *Dark Night of the Soul*, trans. E. Allison Peers (Martino Fine Books, 2017).

7. I love how John O'Donohue encourages us to attend to the inner movements of the heart as sacred invitations to deeper awareness. See John O'Donohue, *Anam Cara: A Book of Celtic Wisdom*, 25th anniversary ed. (Harper Perennial, 2022).
8. Brother Lawrence, *The Practice of the Presence of God*, new abridged ed. (Whitaker House, 1982).
9. This reflection integrates insights from Internal Family Systems (IFS) with the Christian practice of imaginative prayer. See Richard C. Schwartz, *Introduction to the Internal Family Systems Model* (Trailheads, 2001); and Ignatius of Loyola, *The Spiritual Exercises of St. Ignatius: Based on Studies in the Language of the Autograph*, trans. Louis J. Puhl (Loyola University Press, 1951).
10. Kirsten Weir, "The Pain of Social Rejection," *Monitor on Psychology* 43, no. 4 (2012): 50, https://www.apa.org/monitor/2012/04/rejection.
11. M. L. Slepian, et al., "The Experience of Secrecy," *Journal of Personality and Social Psychology* 113, no. 1 (2017):, 1–33, https://psycnet.apa.org/doiLanding?doi=10.1037%2Fpspa0000085.
12. William R. Miller, *On Second Thought: How Ambivalence Shapes Your Life* (Guilford Press, 2022), 6–7.
13. For more on transitional seasons, see Alison Cook, host, *The Best of You*, podcast, episode 88, "Navigating Transitions: What to Do When Change Stirs up Anxiety, Uncertainty, or Confusion," Dr. Alison Cook and Rowena Day, February 1, 2024, https://www.dralisoncook.com/podcasts/navigating-transitions—what-to-do-when-change-stirs-up-anxiety-uncertainty-or-confusion.

ABOUT THE AUTHOR

Dr. Alison Cook is a psychologist of religion, licensed therapist, and host of the top-ranked *The Best of You* podcast. She is the author of several best-selling books, including *Boundaries for Your Soul*. Known for her work at the intersection of faith, psychology, and spiritual formation, she helps people cultivate a secure inner life—healing past wounds, strengthening a grounded sense of self, building healthy relationships, and experiencing God as a steady and loving presence in their lives. She and her husband, Joe, are the parents of two adult children and call both Boston and Wyoming home. Connect with Dr. Alison at www.dralisoncook.com.